KU-297-641

The
Moment of
Ultimate
Breakthrough

Ebenezer Ajitena

EMMANUEL HOUSE
London, United Kingdom

The Moment of Ultimate Breakthrough
Copyright © 2002 by Ebenezer Ajitena

Published by
Emmanuel House
PO Box 15022
London
SE5 7ZL
info@emmanuel-house.org.uk

All Scriptures are taken from the *King James Version* of the Bible.

All rights reserved. No part of this publication may be reproduced, stored in a retrieval system or be transmitted in any form or by any means, mechanical, electronic, photocopying or otherwise without the prior consent of the copyright owner.

ISBN 1 900529 22 X

Cover design by *Himpressions*
Back cover photograph taken by Adeson Productions
Printed in the United Kingdom

CONTENTS

To the Lord of Hosts, Jehovah Saboath,
who has uplifted me throughout
my goings in life, as I embarked
on my journey to the
"Ultimate Breakthrough".

ACKNOWLEDGEMENTS

This book is a product of divine inspiration and leadership of great mentors. Swimming in the ocean of great leaders' wisdom daily, I cannot but express my appreciation to many whose lives have made a tremendous impact in my life.

Space will not permit me to mention all members of *CLIWOM Sanctuary of Praise* who are a great source of support and encouragement.

I would not fail to express my profound and unquantifiable gratitude to my dear wife, Cecilia, and wonderful children for their love, concern and understanding throughout the authorship of this book.

Special thanks to Pastor A.T. Williams, the General Overseer of *God of Glory Christian Centre Worldwide (The Breakthrough Family)*, for his love and support. He has been a source of inspiration and encouragement to me and the entire *CLIWOM Royal Family*.

Special regards also goes to the prayer warriors and workers of *CLIWOM Sanctuary of Praise* for their willingness to serve and their selfless sacrifices.

- Ebenezer Ajitena

INTRODUCTION

Somebody once walked up to me and asked, "Why is life full of ups and downs?" Staring intensely at him, I said, "The life of a Christian is not supposed to be *full* of ups and downs."

Permit me to alter your mindset. What you may regard as the "downs" of life are actually *breakpoints* you have to experience in order to secure a sure *breakthrough*. These *breakpoints* propel you to higher ground.

You were not created for "downs" but for "ups"; God has not destined you for the "bottom seat" but for the "top seat"; you are not to stay "below" but "above". God's desire is to take you to the peak of your destiny, the position of the *Ultimate Breakthrough*.

"And the Lord shall make thee the head, and not the tail; and thou shall be above only, and thou

shalt not be beneath......" (Deut 28:13a).

There is no breakthrough without "breaks". Many people have, indeed, been "broken" on their way to the top and I know you are not an exception. Perhaps someone "broke" your heart or your dreams, visions and ambitions suddenly fell apart; these things do not mean that God is not with you. They are just signposts indicating that you are on the right track to the top.

This book is designed to help you become aware of seven major "breaks" (or signposts) a person must encounter on the way to his ultimate breakthrough. These were exemplified in the life of David; he went through all seven breaks before he finally reached the pinnacle of his life as the "king over Israel".

Watch this:

The "Preliminary Breakthrough zone" is just the start.

The "Break-Out zone" is unavoidable.

The "Break-Away zone" is unbeatable.

The "Break-In zone" is necessary.

The "Break-Off zone" is dynamic.

The "Break-Loose zone" is narrow.

The "Break-Down zone" is dumbfounding.

The "Break-Even zone" is commendable.

But wait a minute.

The "Ultimate Breakthrough zone" is the peak of your journey. It is glorious, superfluous and exhilarating! You cannot beat it—the position of "more than enough!"

Choose Your Destination Today!

You can join this next available flight to the "Ultimate Breakthrough zone" as you delve into the depths of the mystery in this book.

Be strategically positioned as you prepare to be preferred! Pause here. Do not let your "going *through*" affect your "going *to*," for you cannot "go to" unless you "go through.

- Ebenezer Ajitena

DAVID'S BREAKTHROUGH ANALYSIS
(The "7 Breaks" to your "Ultimate Breakthrough")

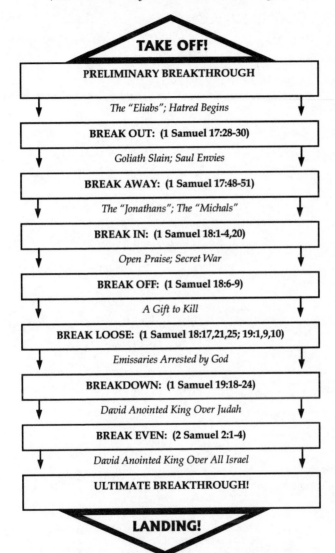

TAKE OFF!

PRELIMINARY BREAKTHROUGH

The "Eliabs"; Hatred Begins

BREAK OUT: (1 Samuel 17:28-30)

Goliath Slain; Saul Envies

BREAK AWAY: (1 Samuel 17:48-51)

The "Jonathans"; The "Michals"

BREAK IN: (1 Samuel 18:1-4,20)

Open Praise; Secret War

BREAK OFF: (1 Samuel 18:6-9)

A Gift to Kill

BREAK LOOSE: (1 Samuel 18:17,21,25; 19:1,9,10)

Emissaries Arrested by God

BREAKDOWN: (1 Samuel 19:18-24)

David Anointed King Over Judah

BREAK EVEN: (2 Samuel 2:1-4)

David Anointed King Over All Israel

ULTIMATE BREAKTHROUGH!

LANDING!

*When you attain your ultimate breakthrough,
enemies can no longer handle you.
So do not stop halfway; aim for the ultimate moment
(2 Samuel 5:17).*

THE BEGINNING OF SUCCESS

(The Preliminary Breakthrough Zone)

Before you attain your ultimate breakthrough in life, you will, inevitably, encounter seven breaks. Your journey will start from a place I call the preliminary breakthrough zone.

The preliminary breakthrough zone is the point where you experience little drops of God's abundance and small doors of success open before you. At this point, God begins to show you glimpses of what He has in stock for you.

Unfortunately, many people never make progress towards their ultimate breakthrough because they do not know how to manage their preliminary breakthroughs. They settle at the beginning of success when there are greater heights to attain.

What are the things that happen at the preliminary breakthrough phase? How must you respond to people's opinions of you at this stage? What are the necessary things to do in order to move on to higher heights? Much insight can be found in the life of David.

David at the Beginning of Success

God told Samuel that He had prepared a king for Israel to replace Saul. He told the prophet that the future king would be one of Jesse's children. With this revelation, Samuel took the anointing oil and proceeded to Jesse's house to locate the Lord's chosen.

When Samuel got to Jesse's house, he realised that his task was not that straightforward; seven sons of Jesse lined up in front of him to be chosen as king! David, who was the chosen of God, was despised by men — he was not even called to join the procession.

Although David was young in age, his spirit was well built and mature. In the sight of men he was incapable but in God's sight he was more than able. This was the beginning of David's journey to breakthrough.

"And it came to pass, when they were come, he looked on Eliab and said, Surely the Lord's anointed is before him. But the Lord said unto Samuel, Look not on his countenance, or on the height of his stature; because I have refused him: for the Lord seeth not as man seeth; for man looketh at the outward appearance but the Lord looketh at the heart. Then Jesse called Abinadab and made him pass before Samuel and said, neither hath the Lord chosen these. And Samuel said unto Jesse, Are here all thy children? And he said, There remaineth yet the youngest, and, behold, he keepeth the sheep. And Samuel said unto Jesse, Send and fetch him: for we will not sit down till he come hither" (1 Samuel 16:6-11).

It is possible for a minister of God to have wrong assumptions about people. Samuel made a wrong judgment about Eliab and God had to correct him.

The truth is that David was already appointed by God before Samuel got to Jesse's house and Samuel's error could not change God's preordained counsel.

Before your today, God has already chosen you for success. God is taking you to a predetermined place of greatness. You are on your way to breakthroughs and you should not stay too long in transit.

Nobody has the power to speak negatively into your life because it is too late; God has already concluded your story. He conceals the end of a thing from the beginning thereof. Before you set out on the journey, God already concluded everything for you. Before you start, God has finished. Whatever you need for every aspect of your life has been planned by God.

Nobody knows the exact mind of God about your life. It is the Spirit of God that connects a man to his divine destiny because the bible says, "Eyes hath not seen, ears have not heard, neither has it entered the mind of man what God has prepared for those who love him." (I Corinthians 2:9).

Approved by God; Refused by Man

When Samuel saw Eliab's height and stature, he thought Eliab was the chosen king, but God said *"Look not on his outward countenance or on the height of his stature because I have refused him."*

At the preliminary breakthrough stage, you must be patient and calm. Take time to study your environment and the people around you before making important, life-changing decisions. A premature conclusion about what God is saying can prove disastrous.

It is not wise, for instance, to rush into buying something if all your money will be spent on the purchase. You need to think about maintenance and reserve some money for that purpose. If it is not time to broadcast your achievements, be quiet about them. You are still at the preliminary breakthrough stage. Take into account what your expenses will be under the preliminary breakthrough so you do not walk under false prosperity. If you walk under false prosperity, people who should genuinely help you will withdraw because they will have a false impression about you.

Check Your Passengers

You should not go around with people who do not share your vision. If the people on your vehicle of destiny are not going to the same address as yours, then drop them off. If you carry people who are not going to your destination, you may never reach your own destination. You will be distracted because they will divert your attention. Their attention is towards where *they* are going and yours is on where *you* are going. If someone does not have anything to contribute to your success, drop him off. Until Lot departed to Sodom, Abraham could not progress into the promised land.

If you have to run your leadership by virtue of what people will say and the opinions of others then you are not a leader. If you cannot decide on what God has said concerning your life then you cannot make progress.

Preliminary breakthroughs give the blueprint of where you are going. God will show you the way but He will not break the wrong people off you. You should know who to take and who not to take. You must check who is in the vehicle of your destiny.

If you have the wrong people, do not start the journey because wrong people cause delays. Never be too kind with someone who is negative about your destiny. These are some of the things to do at your preliminary breakthrough zone.

Watch Out for Eliab

Your "Eliab" will always show up before your "David". David is the chosen, but Eliab is the reject. Eliab does not want to know that he is rejected because he feels no one else in the family can be chosen other than him.

There is always an Eliab that feels he is indispensable. Never feel you are indispensable because everyone has a place in the kingdom of God. David was abandoned in the wilderness but God still found him out. God had a unique place for David to occupy.

Samuel asked for David and everyone had to stand on their feet until he came! When it is time for you to flourish, people will rush to acknowledge you. They will not rest until you are blessed. God will order a lifting for you in Jesus' name.

Young but Chosen

"And he sent and they brought him in. Now he was ruddy, and withal of a beautiful countenance, and goodly to look to. And the Lord said, Arise, anoint him: for this is he." (1 Samuel 16:12)

When Samuel tried pouring the oil to anoint Eliab, the oil did not flow. It did not flow over the seven brothers because God does not waste His grace. But when the preferred David came, the oil was released.

David was the last but yet became first. Your position in the family cannot hinder what God wants to do in your life. God can use you to alter the history of your family; He will make it happen through you and kings shall come to the brightness of your rising (Isaiah 60:3).

Be careful when men attempt to raise you up. If they raise you they can soon erase you. When God raises you, He has the power to sustain you.

Open Exaltation

"Then Samuel took the horn of oil and anointed him in the midst of his brethren and the spirit of God came upon David from that day forward."

God anointed David in the midst of his brethren; he was lifted up in the midst of those who previously looked down on him.

From the day you are anointed for the appointed time, the Spirit of the Lord falls mightily on you and you will begin to see issues of your life in a different light. It is of more importance for you to have God's perspective about life than man's perspective.

Your Eliabs will not want you to fully accomplish God's design and purposes despite all your efforts to bless them. Nothing will make them love you. The Eliabs will never be satisfied. There might be an Eliab in your family and you are trying so much to please him. No amount of money that you give can please such a person. Eliab is always bitter against the Lord's anointed.

Eliab's Opposition—The Breakout Zone

"And Eliab his eldest brother heard when he spake unto the men; and Eliab's anger was kindled against David, and he said, Why camest thou down hither? And with whom has thou left those few sheep? I know thy pride, and the naughtiness of thy heart; for thou art come down that thou mightest see the battle." (1 Samuel 17:28).

Even after the open pronouncements on David's life, Eliab still underrated David. He did not want David to see the battle talk less of fight in it. Notwithstanding, the driving force of destiny moved David into the camp and he heard the soldiers talking about the reward to be given to anyone who could fight and defeat Goliath. David's inquisitiveness angered Eliab. He coveted David's anointing and did not want any attention focused on the little, shepherd boy.

Listen, when you are at the level of your preliminary breakthrough, some of your good friends, relatives and colleagues will have to break out because of their inability to accept the fact that you will be made king over them.

David was ready to take a bold step that no-one else was ready to take. He was ready to take risks and with such a resolution, he distinguished himself from the fearful. Lovers of comfort are not always comfortable around risk-takers and if they cannot dissuade the risk-taker, they will try to hinder him.

Nobody can hinder your initiatives because your life is hid in Christ and the destiny for your life is intact in God. At your preliminary breakthrough, make up your mind to stay focused on God. Hear from Him and obey Him accordingly. Do not allow sin into your life at this stage because sin will hinder your fellowship with God and cut the flow of His power into your life. As a risk-taker you need to be in touch with God. The Spirit of God must be on you so that you can break out of mediocrity and from the grip of your Eliabs.

Do not send your resources to Eliabs because they will use them to attack you. God destined David to lead the future generation but Eliab wanted him to remain in the wilderness. When you are over-excited about your opportunities, take your time to identify whom you are sharing your progress with. You do not need to announce it; the result will speak for itself. When your breakthrough comes, you can no longer hide it, because people will come and try to reconcile with you. Wait for God's time; do not arrive before your arrival.

Is There Not a Cause?

"And David said, what have I now done? Is there not a cause?" (1 Samuel 17:29).

Is there not a reason why you are the pastor of that church? Is there not a reason why God did not allow the enemy to kill you till now? Is there not a cause for your being in the house of God? Is there not a cause for you to face the battles of life instead of run from them?

There is a reason for everything you are going through in life; there is a cause for which your destiny must be fulfilled. You are the solution to someone's problems. Jesus is the reason and the cause for your existence and through Him, you ought to bring meaning into the problems of people around you.

Break Out!

"And he turned from him towards another, and spake after the same manner: and the people answered him again after the former manner." (1 Samuel 17:30)

At the break out point, you may need to separate from some family members that are hanging around you before you can make any significant progress towards success. You may need to end some relationships in order to consolidate your relationship with God. Perhaps your business needs reorganisation or your marriage needs a retreat or the system of running your family needs adjustment. Whatever is necessary for progress in your life must be done without any compromise.

David turned away from his brother. You may need to turn away and break out of some relationships. If you have relatives that are running you down, it is better you break out of the relationships. It is better you send them off so you can move forward.

This was the point of David's preliminary breakthrough. At this point, members of his family had to break out. It was a total break out, so do not feel bad when you are sidetracked, God Himself may orchestrate it. Do not feel bad when people reject you; it is a dynamic mobility to your destiny. Even Jesus was rejected.

The level at which people can understand what you are up to depends on how you can relate it to them. You cannot see the magnitude of your vision at a go. As you run with the vision, it will expand. You have to start from somewhere. Start from where you are.

People do not want to identify with the level you are when you start but when success comes, everyone will claim you as a member of their family. Stay focused with God until your breakthrough comes.

WISDOM PRINCIPLES

Visions are caught and not taught;
only the people who can catch your vision
will flow with it.

You are the best manager of your life;
someone else cannot see what you see
the way you see it.

People heading for a destination different from yours
need not be in your vehicle of destiny.
Check who is in your vehicle to avoid distraction on
your way to success.

If someone does not have anything to
contribute to you at the beginning of success
then drop him off.

If you are influenced by what people say and what
their opinion are, then you are not a leader.

Never be too kind with someone who is negative
about your destiny. You must fight the course
and let him fall apart.

*The enemy of your success will be
put on attention until you are enthroned.*

*The enemy that wants to take your place
will be the errand boy to call you for
your appointment.*

*Do not release the information of where you are going
to the Eliabs lest they fight you with the piece of
information they receive from you.*

*Many people are Eliabs —
they look kingly but they are not actually kings.*

*Your Eliab will not want you to fully
accomplish God's design and purposes despite all your
efforts to bless them.*

*When you are at the level of your
preliminary breakthrough, some of your good friends,
relatives and colleagues will have to break out because
they will not be able to conceive the fact
that you will be made king over them.*

*Eliab will always want David to remain
in the wilderness tending sheep when David is
anointed to deliver a nation.*

*The level at which people can understand
what you are up to depends on how
you can relate it to them.*

*You cannot see the magnitude of your vision at a go.
As you continue in it, it will expand.*

*The scars of destiny are there to remind you of the
things that have happened to you.*

*If it comes from man, you will have to pay man for it
but if it comes from God, you do not owe man
anything.*

*The degree of effort the devil puts in motion
to stop you is an indication of your
coming breakthrough.*

*Never allow people's reaction to dictate
the fulfillment of your dream.*

*See your vision; speak your vision
and add value to your dream.*

MILE TWO

FACING THE
STANDING GIANT
(The Break-Away Zone)

Y our journey towards destiny should have a successful end. This is the plan of God for you. However, on your way to your ultimate breakthrough you will always meet a giant. After you overcome the Eliabs of your destiny, your next battle is with the Goliaths.

Goliath is the giant that stands between you and your ultimate breakthrough. Goliath is more dangerous than Eliab. Goliath is ready to defy the God in whom you believe; his main goal is to bring the glory, integrity, and character of your God to disrepute.

If you are presently facing a long-standing, severe trial, there is a Goliath before you. Every situation that tries your faith and wants you to doubt God's ability is a Goliath. There is a Goliath that wants to stand against your success, future, marriage and destiny.

The Enemy of Completion

God made everyone for a purpose. When you recognise the purpose of God for your life, you are motivated to pursue it. For every purpose there must be a pursuit. Your pursuit is your goal, vision and dream. There cannot be any fulfillment of purpose without a pursuit.

Goliath knows that God has a purpose for your life but he wants to intimidate you so that you would not accomplish the purpose and vision of God for your life. God is a God of vision and purpose. He does not want you only to start your journey towards greatness, but also to finish successfully. If you are not ready to persevere to the end of what you are pursuing, do not start the pursuit at all. Goliath is the enemy that wants to prevent you from enduring to the end. He will always meet you halfway and attempt to stop you in your tracks.

Big Problems Require Great Determination

Goliath can represent any big problem in your life. The Goliath that David faced was 12 ft tall! Is there a problem in your life that looks impossible to handle or control? It is nothing but a Goliath, and if David destroyed his Goliath you can destroy yours too.

There is no mountain on the earth that man cannot climb, no desert he cannot cross — if he sets his heart to do it, holding his life in his hands, ready to keep it or lose it as heaven may order.

This is an ultimate determination you must have when facing Goliath. The only people who are not confronted by anything are those in the grave. As long as there is life in you, there is hope. So, do not give up before the fight. Make up your mind to confront your giant. There is nothing like a journey without confrontation. So long as you are destined for greatness, the enemy will meet you halfway.

You started your journey of success from the beginning to the end but the enemy started his from the end to meet you halfway. He knows that if you maintain your present pace unhindered, you will make it.

The enemy knows that you have an expected end. Whatever you see in your life right now is *not* your expected end. You are just on transit to your ultimate breakthrough. Until you fight and bring down the Goliath in your life your fame will not be known.

Will This Mountain Move?

There is no reason to be afraid of what you cannot avoid to confront. Why should you be afraid when God has ordained this for you? God knows that when you defeat Goliath everyone will marvel at the potential in you. He is the one who has set you up for this battle so you need not be afraid.

Some trials are ordained in your life to perfect your faith. You can never be perfect unless you face trials from the tempter. God will not prevent the trial. Instead, He will see you through by passing through it *with* you. He will not remove the fiery furnace of your journey but will lead you *through* it.

No amount of prayer can remove the mountain you *must* climb. God will not remove it for you. He will give you power to endure and overcome it. Jesus went through the cross because he had to. In prayer, the Lord requested for the cup of suffering to pass over him, but He later surrendered totally to the will of God: "Not my will but yours be done."

This means that some cups of pain will not pass over you but God will give you the grace to endure them. Not all mountains are meant to be removed. If the mountain will not be moved then the Lord will strengthen you to overtop it.

When you discover your wings then the Lord will empower you to soar over every temptation in Jesus' name.

Unction on the Skill

When David faced Goliath, his skills were instrumental in the victory he attained. He identified his skill and the anointing of God empowered it for victory. God's unction will always multiply the output of your skill. In other words, you have to be skillful. You have to identify what you can do and then rely on the anointing of God to show it forth.

For instance, it was David's skill on the harp that singled him out as a temporary solution to Saul's problem. Every time he played the instrument, he played with gentility and grace. His music was acceptable before the Lord and the anointing backed it up.

Any skill that is tainted with pride cannot be accepted by God. It might be accepted, applauded and appreciated by people and still be rejected by God. Only the praise that is backed up by humility is acceptable. Each time David played, the evil spirit that troubled Saul left. Entertainment is different from worship; David did not entertain Saul but worshipped God.

David's skill with a sling was the weapon God used to defeat Goliath. On the road to your ultimate breakthrough, make sure you sharpen your skills so that when God's anointing is on you, victory will be certain.

The Borrowed Armour

"And Saul armed David with his armour, and he put an helmet of brass upon his head." (I Samuel 17:37-38).

Saul attempted to distract David from his skills by arming him with untested weapons. These weapons did not work for Saul against Goliath so how could they work for David? By clothing David with his armour, Saul was automatically preparing David for failure.

You must be careful before whom you stand when you are preparing for the journey of destiny. Do not borrow ideas from the rejected. Do not let anyone under a closed heaven close your own heaven for you. Do not let anyone who has no business with what God has put in your life speak into your life.

Saul, the rejected, was trying to prepare David, the accepted, for a journey that will lead to the heights of fame. Saul armed David but what kind of clothing can you get from someone who is rejected by God?

Components of Saul's Armour

"And he put an helmet of brass upon his head;" (1 Samuel 17:38).

Note that Saul did not give David an helmet of salvation but an *helmet of "brass"*. Brass is a sign of closed heaven: "And the heaven that is above thy head shall be *brass*" (Deuteronomy 28:23).

Do not expect any help from people that God has not ordained to be helpers in your life. Do not rely on what men promise to do for you and thus put yourself under their bondage. When the enemy puts a helmet of brass on your head, your mentality is limited and your thinking is messed up. It will become difficult for you to make right decisions.

There are some things that God expects you to do in order to progress, but when the enemy limits you with a helmet of brass, you cannot use your initiatives properly. You should not expect a miracle for something God has given you the wisdom to do. Disallow, therefore, the helmet of brass on your head and retain your free thinking and initiative.

"Also armed him with a coat of mail." (1 Samuel 17:38).

A *coat of mail* is a coat of iron that does not allow for freshness or the penetration of anything good. Joseph was clothed with a coat of many colours but Saul armed David with a coat of iron. In that coat of iron, you are stuck and you are not allowed to experience the goodness of a new day. Do not allow Saul to put a coat of mail on you. You should also never be an obstruction in anybody's life so that nobody will obstruct you too.

"And David girded his sword upon his armour, and he assayed to go; for he had not proved it. And David said unto Saul, I cannot go with these for I have not proved them. And David put them off." (1 Samuel 17:39).

What you have not tried or tested will not do you any good. Do not follow the crowd or borrow people's ideas to run your life. That an idea works for someone else does not mean it will work for you. So put off the heavy armour of Saul and be free to be yourself. You do not need to borrow ideas because you are full of ideas.

All-Round Restriction

After David was armed by Saul he could not move an inch. This means he could not make any progress in the journey of life. David was hindered by Saul's armour.

David did not reject the idea of being armed but the armour harmed him. The presence of the rejected in your life can stagnate your journey. Any attempt to move will be difficult.

It is possible to be filled with the anointing and yet have Saul-like people cover it up. I know you have the anointing of God upon your life, but what are you wearing on it? You cannot put on the cloth of abomination belonging to someone who wants to lord over you and expect success. If the anointing is in your life and you entangle yourself with anything that is carrying a curse, you will be stagnated and rendered immobile. Be careful; do not let "Saul" arm you for battle.

You cannot fight your battle with unfamiliar protection. If you do, who will you give glory if you win the battle — to the rejected Saul or to the King of glory?

I do not know if you are under the influence of other people who have been ruling you, it is better you pull out now and refuse to stay there. Perhaps you have been trying to influence someone in an attempt to teach them what to do in their homes. Such attempts are manifestations of Saul's spirit.

Do not superimpose your will on others. Do not try to put your armour on someone because you will disturb their ability to move freely. If you want your daughter to get married do not try to dress her with an armour that will get her stagnated and hinder her from getting to her destination. If you cannot take a decision unless you consult everybody then you are under Saul's armour. If you take Saul's armour then you are relegating the power of God in your life and His ability to do whatever He likes. You should never live under the control of a person that is not receiving instructions from God. Who is your mentor? Who speaks into your life?

So many people are in a place while their control tower is in another place — with someone else who controls them in another location. Even if you are anointed but you are under Saul's armour, you cannot make any impact; you may have the living word but you cannot leave the place you are. You are limited, barricaded and hindered.

There is nothing you can do to pacify someone who hates you. If David had taken Saul's armour, Saul would have shared in the glory that belonged to God and would have attributed the victory to the power in his armour. He would have challenged David and would have told David that his armour made him win over Goliath.

Do not fight your battles with borrowed instruments. Use whatever you have and rely on the power of God in your life to be the ultimate for you. Never relax or venture to move under the armour of Saul.

No matter what Goliath is saying in your life, you are a victor through Christ. Goliath will always come to frighten you but the bible says, "fear not" (Isaiah 7:4). If the Greater One is in you then you have no reason to be afraid of anything. Psalms 27:1 says that the Lord is your light and salvation, whom shall you fear and the Lord is the Lord of your life, of whom shall you be afraid?

God will see you through if you rely on Him and not on Saul's armour.

Free to Advance!

"And he took his staff in his hand, and chose him five smooth stones out of the brook, and put them in a shepherd's bag which he had, even in a scrip; and his sling was in his hand: and he drew near to the philistines." (1 Samuel 17:40)

David refused Saul's armour and took what he was used to—a little sling. It was not big in the eyes of man but David was used to it and with it he could advance towards Goliath.

What is that "little thing", that little idea, that you have in your life? You can move forward with it and trust God for a breakthrough. It may seem small but God can use it to bring down the mighty.

Be confident and competent with the little sling God has given you. Also be determined to bring down this standing Goliath in your life. It may be the Goliath of inferiority or the Goliath of sickness or the Goliath of death or the Goliath of failure. Whatever this Goliath represents in your life, locate it and use your sling to defeat it.

Aim Well and Aim High!

Every part of Goliath was fully covered with iron except his forehead. David targeted this exposed and unprotected area when he aimed at Goliath. You would need to aim well and high at you Goliath in order to kill it.

God directed the stone to Goliath's forehead because the head is very important; it coordinates every part of the body. When David released the stone, God empowered it for Goliath's destruction.

Do not be frightened by the bigness of your Goliath. All you need is the small space on his forehead.

David did not rely on himself; he relied on God. He fought and defeated Goliath with the power of God.

You can start your business with the little capital you have. It does not matter how small it is; just trust in God and be determined to bring down the standing giant.

I know the problem in your life looks and feels insurmountable but listen, you should look beyond the problem and see the God that controls the problem.

Battle of the gods

There is a secret you need to understand from David's victory over Goliath. Something happened when David and Goliath met each other.

When David saw Goliath, he did not see the bigness of Goliath but he saw the bigness of the God of Israel in himself.

When Goliath saw David, he did not just see a little lad; he recognised that David was not an ordinary boy. Under normal circumstances, Goliath would have been put off by David's size, but he saw more than a small boy; he saw the God of Israel in David.

The truth is that there was a spiritual battle going on; the two gods recognised themselves — the God of the Israelites and the god of the philistines, and because David believed in the God of Israel, he won the battle. The battle was not based on the size of human beings but on the ability of the gods at war.

From now on, you should not focus on the bigness of your problem but focus on the smallness of the devil and the bigness of God. If you perceive your trials in this light, you will bring down the standing giant.

From Rejected to Accepted

After Goliath was destroyed, news about David's victory spread abroad. The people recognised God's grace on David. They started to see David as a replacement for Saul.

Saul, who was once accepted by the people, was rejected by God, and David, who was once rejected by his brothers, began to find acceptance with the people. For every Saul there is always a David. David is the accepted and preferred but Saul is the rejected.

David was able to cross another milestone in his journey towards ultimate breakthrough. The Spirit of God came upon him "from that day forward" and he progressed in the anointing.

God's anointing is upon you. Do not let anything contaminate it. Saul's anointing as king left him and he forfeited his moment of ultimate breakthrough. David moved on and reached his destination.

You have a destination too. If you are focused and determined you will reach your ultimate breakthrough. This is God's will for you.

WISDOM PRINCIPLES

For every purpose there must be a pursuit.
There cannot be any fulfillment of purpose
without pursuit.

There is no mountain upon the earth that man cannot
climb; no desert he cannot cross – if he sets his heart to
doing it.

There must be an ultimate determination
for one to experience an ultimate breakthrough.

There is a divine force that attracts the enemy to try
everyone in pursuit of purpose.

You started your journey of success from the
beginning to the end but the enemy started his from
the end to meet you halfway.

No amount of prayer can remove the
mountains you must climb.

Do not fight your battle with a
borrowed instrument.

Strange armour brings strange burden.

Be confident with your "Sling Shot"
and aim well.

God will not charge you with a responsibility for
which you have no experience.

You should never expect a miracle for something
God has given you the wisdom to do.

Do not borrow people's ideas to run your life,
because it worked for someone does not mean it will
work for you.

Do not focus on the bigness of your problem;
Focus instead on the smallness of the devil and the
bigness of God.

You can never escape a problem by avoiding it.

Whenever you are labeled or described by
the future you are yet to possess, don't resist it.

You may hit the bottom of the pit, but don't be afraid,
your next move is up.

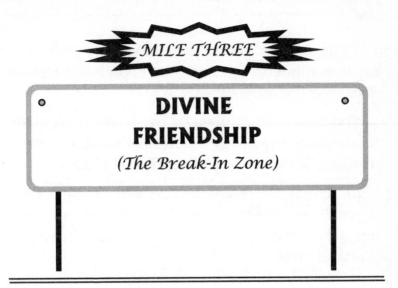

DIVINE FRIENDSHIP
(The Break-In Zone)

The Law of Relationship

Friendship is very important in the life of anyone journeying towards an ultimate breakthrough. God made us with an in-built desire for friendship and companionship. God does not want man to be alone. He wants us to dwell in the company of others.

By saying it was not good for man to be alone, God was establishing the law of relationship. This law functions in such a way that no matter where man finds himself, he will always seek for someone with whom he can relate.

There is nobody that does not desire to have a relationship with someone else. God has made us dependent on each other.

You are either influenced by people or you are influencing others. Relationships always have a measure of influence on the affected parties.

In whatever relationship you might find yourself, be sure that the relationship is influencing you positively and you are influencing it positively too.

The Power of Friendship

If God wants to do something in your life, it will usually come through someone. When the enemy wants to send a breakdown into ones life, it also comes through people. This means that care must be taken to ascertain the kind of people you relate with. Your friend can determine your strength or weakness. "He that worketh with wise men shall be wise but a companion of fools shall be destroyed" (Proverbs 13:20).

Meeting the right person at the right time is very important. Through such divine meetings, God can connect you to the place where you are supposed to be. The right person may not come from a place you expect, so be open to God and do not miss your divine moment.

If you will get to your ultimate breakthrough, some rearrangement and readjustment may be necessary. Some people will *painfully* get out of your life while some others will *easily* get out. There is no way a parasite leaves a tree without leaving a mark; there is no way some people will be cut off from your life without leaving a mark on your flesh. Some departures of people will bring pain. However, in this mile, God will cut off every connection that will not glorify Him. God will cut off all wrong relationships so that He can get your full attention. Remember, He is a jealous God.

You Need Closed Doors

Everyone prays for open doors but sometimes we need some open doors to close. Not every door that you find open is from God. There are some doors that the enemy opens to cause confusion. Do not settle for less than the best.

You need closed doors in order to give God total concentration. Doors that are not opened by God will not allow the right doors to open up. Many people are struggling and suffering because they have gone through doors that have been opened by the enemy. There are some doors that are used as distractions to alter your concentration from God. They serve as alternative routes to your destiny and your vision. They are counterfeits of progress.

Your Friends are Your Packaging

Whoever you relate with will have a lasting impact on your life. Many people might not have the opportunity to meet you but they can meet you through the lives of the people you have reached either positively or negatively. Your friends are your packaging. People can predict who you are just by looking at your friends. This is possible because like-minded people relate with together. People who do not have similar mindsets do not have much of a relationship with each other.

You can miss great opportunities by packaging the right substance with the wrong wrap. Your package determines your worth, your worth determines your value and your value determines your virtue.

It is important, therefore, that you are with the right people because people will rate you based on the relationships you keep. You will be addressed by the way you dress; and your friends are the dress you put on.

By Choice and Not By Force

When you relate with the wrong set of people, you cannot get to your destination. Make sure you do not travel on the right track with the wrong people .

Friendship is by choice and not by force. You should choose who you make friends with. Stay away from a fool so that you too will not become a fool. Fools cannot teach you anything worthwhile. If there is nothing that you gain from a friend either morally or spiritually, then you do not have a friend but a fiend.

You must be careful because much havoc is caused by *fiends* who tear down friends; people who use the little information they have about a person to tear others down. You must stay away from people who will not contribute to your success. "Go from the presence of a foolish man, when thou perceiveth not in him the lips of knowledge (Proverbs 14:7).

Stay Away From Fools

I cannot overstate this counsel. This stage in your life is crucial as you journey towards your ultimate breakthrough. The bible warns that if you want to make it in life, be careful in choosing your friends. You must stay away from fools. If you want good advice make sure you have the right set of friends because an advice can unlock your destiny or ruin it forever.

God will not make you stay away from the bad company but you have to help yourself and choose who you walk with.

Whoever you walk with determines whom you talk with and whom you talk with determines whom you will be connected with.

Bad-Tempered Friends

Being quick-tempered is different from being bad-tempered. When a person is quick-tempered, he is easily roused but when a person is bad-tempered then he is unreasonable and cantankerous. Such a person cannot be satisfied because he always looks down on others. A bad-tempered person is uncomfortable with the progress of people around him.

God warns that we should stay away from quick-tempered and bad-tempered people.

"Make no friendship with an angry man; and with a furious man thou shalt not go: lest thou learn his ways, and get a snare to thy soul." (Proverbs 22:24-25)

Some people are bad-tempered but they are not quick-tempered. The bad-tempered person does not want your progress in life. You must be ready to make adjustments on your relationships. Do not stay a minute more with either bad or quick tempered people.

Unreliable Friends

"Confidence in an unfaithful man in time of trouble is like a broken tooth, and a foot out of joint." (Proverbs 25:19)

Be careful of open gratification so that you can have a lasting glorification.

Do not put yourself in the hands of an unreliable man. It can be very disastrous. Remember, friends can have negative or positive impacts on you.

Unreliable friends are very dangerous because you will not even know when you are on the right track and when you are on the wrong track. They are very deceptive and can be dangerously misleading.

God-Given Friends

"Ointment and perfume rejoice the heart; so doth the sweetness of a man's friend by hearty counsel." (Proverbs 27:9)

If you have a friend that gives you the right counsel and connects you to the right authority and rejoices in your elevation, such a friend is like ointment and perfume.

The essence of perfume is that it beautifies the life of those who posses it. Such is the effect of God-given friends. When you have good friends, your life will be beautified. Many lives are ugly and shapeless because they are in the wrong relationships.

God-given friends are also like ointment and the essence of ointment is to lubricate. You can prevent your life and ministry from becoming rusty by nurturing the right kind of friendship.

There are people who seek just what they can get out of you without seeking what they can do to help. They only seek to receive without any desire to give. Good friends are not concerned about what they can get but rather what they can give. When you have the right kind of friends, your life will always be lubricated and smooth.

A good friend does not want you to dwell on past glory, but keeps pushing you to make progress. Thank God for the many prayers that have been answered in your life. You need a friend that will celebrate with you in the now and also stir you up to greater achievements.

The friendship David had with Jonathan was a divine, God-ordained relationship. It helped David immensely on his journey towards his ultimate breakthrough.

Jonathan

"And it came to pass, when he had made an end of speaking unto Saul that the soul of Jonathan was knit with the soul of David, and Jonathan loved him as his own soul" (1 Samuel 18:1).

This is the kind of divine friendship you should desire. After you have overcome the Eliabs of your life and defeated the Goliaths, then you must find out who is helping you. This is the level of Breaking-In. The bible says that the soul of Jonathan was knit to the soul of David and they both became covenant friends by God's divine plan and purpose.

Wherever there is divine friendship there is genuine love. Jonathan's kind of love is the kind

God expects us to have for our brethren. It is the kind of love that is ready to do anything for a friend, even the giving of one's life.

Jonathan, Not Jonadab

Jonathan is different from Jonadab

Jonathan means *Jehovah has given.*

Jonadab means *Jehovah gives.*

Jonathan means that God has already *given* all that we need, while Jonadab means the Lord *will give* if you ask (and if you do not ask then you will not receive).

Jonathan was a friend to David while Jonadab was a friend to Amnon (2 Samuel 13:1-15). Amnon consulted Jonadab about his feelings towards his sister, Tamar. He sought counsel on how he could lie with her. Jonadab thought him an evil plan which led Amnon to rape his sister.

Amnon received and followed an advice from a fool. However, it brought him under a generational curse and he paid for his folly through the wrath of Absalom.

Amnon's friend, Jonadab, was a crafty and foolish person. David's friend, Jonathan, on the other hand, was a friend indeed. Watch out for the person you share your life with.

Divinely Connected

David's relationship with Jonathan was a covenant friendship and such only comes about by divine connection. God planted a love between them so that Jonathan could reveal all the evils that Saul was planning against David.

If everyone in your family hates you, God will sometimes make the soul of one member of the family to knit to yours so that the trap people set would be exposed.

There will always be a Jonathan in the life of every David. The Jonathan of your life is the person who celebrates you at every point of success and inconveniences himself to see that you succeed.

The Greatest Friend of All

The greatest friend we could ever have is God who sent His Son to come and pay the price for our salvation. Your victory over the trials of life is not because of your perfection; it is the love and mercy of God that has kept you.

A good environment does not beautify your life. Get your priorities right: only Jesus is a friend that will never disappoint you. He gave His life as a ransom for all. Greater love hath no man than this, that a man should lay down his life for His friends (John 15:13).

You do not have the power to make a good contact unless the Lord directs you. What you call the best may turn out to be the worst. The friends you need are only those directed by God. These are people who are ready to inconvenience themselves to please you.

If you have Jesus Christ as a friend, He will guide you through the "breaks" on the way to your ultimate breakthrough.

WISDOM PRINCIPLES

Make sure you are not on the right track with the wrong people.

Friendship is by choice and not by force; choose who you make friends with.

If there is nothing that you gain from a person, either morally or spiritually, then he is not a friend but a fiend.

The people you walk with determine the people you talk with and the people you talk with determine the people you will be connected with.

Be careful of open gratification so that you can have a lasting glorification.

There is no way a parasite can leave a tree without leaving a mark. Likewise, some friends will have to leave you painfully.

The greatest wickedness can hide
under the mask of piety.

You cannot survive the challenges of life
without God, and your survival is a living proof that
God is the best friend you could ever have.

The people who speak into your life have
great impact upon you.

There will always be a Jonathan
in the life of every David.

Your package determines your worth,
your worth determines your value and
your value determines your virtue.

You will be addressed the way you dress;
your friends are the dress you put on.

MILE FOUR

BEWARE
OF TRAPS
(The Break-Off Zone)

As you prepare to *appear* before the pharaoh of your vision, be ready to *disappear* before the Saul of your destiny.

A trap is a dangerous vice concealed from the view of its victim. The devil usually seeks to ensnare people's lives through traps. A trap is a subtle scheme of the devil.

A trap takes people unawares in a subtle manner. No-one will sees a snare and knowingly fall into it. Traps catch people because they were ignorant of its presence.

Trap-setters usually lure their victims to the strategic place the trap has been hid. Without any doubt, the enemy is actively seeking how to entrap you and destroy your purpose in God.

The enemy of purpose sets his eyes on the children of promise and on those who are on the road to greatness. The enemy is interested in people destined to make a mark for God and he sets his eyes on them for evil. Are you surprised that the devil is making many attempts against your life and purpose? It is because of the treasures that God has put in you; treasures that are ordained for the devil's defeat. Thank God the bible says that *"our soul is escaped like a bird out of the snare of the fowler and the snare is broken and I am escaped"* (Psalm 126:5).

A Snare After Victory

David had passed three different stages on his way to the throne: he side-stepped Eliabs, defeated Goliath and befriended Jonathan. At the height of victory, the devil set a trap for him. Consider the life of David in the passage below:

"And it came to pass as they came, when David was returned from the slaughter of the Philistine, that the women came out of all the cities of Israel, singing and dancing, to meet king Saul, with

*tabrets, with joy, and with instruments of
musick. And the women answered one another as
they played, and said, Saul hath slain his
thousands, and David his ten thousands. And
Saul was very wroth and the saying displeased
him; and he said, They have ascribed unto David
ten thousands, and to me they have ascribed but
thousands: and what can he have more but the
kingdom? And Saul eyed David from that day
forward" (1 Samuel 18:6-9).*

Open praise and public ovation are dangerous
especially when those who are losing their fame
at the beginning of yours are there to witness
your praise.

Many things we call blessings today are traps.
You need to be in control of yourself when you
see things that glitter but are not gold. If you must
fulfill your destiny and reach your ultimate breakthrough, you must avoid snares on your way.

Saul eyed David from that day forward (after
the defeat of Goliath). He grudged David and at
the same time wanted David to stay in the palace.
It is possible for you to be in the palace of your
enemy; if you do not escape quickly, you will
likely lose your life. Joseph's brothers decided to
kill him and his dreams. Be careful not to relax in
the camp of the enemy.

Divine Replacement

David, the anointed, was on his way to the throne and to the heights of fame but Saul was on his way to destruction. Before God replaced Saul, He had already prepared David. Whatever God has given to you should be done with haste and urgency. God will rather replace man than allow His work to halt. God can replace anybody. No-one is indispensable before God. He replaced Saul with David.

Saul envied David intensely. His thoughts concerning the young warrior were evil continually. Be ready to celebrate the progress of others. If you do not celebrate others, you will not be celebrated. Stop deliberating about others and start celebrating them. There is no reason to eye someone else when God can do even greater things in your own life.

The Deadly Gift: Break-Loose Zone

David had God's promise but he did not discuss it with Saul. He knew how to overcome Goliath but he did not share the secret with Saul. He only shared his past experiences; he did not reveal the secret behind the "sling shot". As a result, Saul could not understand or stop the favour on David's life.

Be on your guard when you are moving towards your ultimate breakthrough. There is always a snare around. Saul, full of jealousy and envy, attempted to entrap David with a gift.

"And Saul said to David, Behold my elder Daughter Merab, her will I give thee to wife: only be thou valiant for me and fight the Lord's battles. For Saul said Let not mine hand be upon him, but let the hand of the Philistines be upon him" (1 Samuel 18:17)

There is a gift to heal and there is a gift to kill. This gift of marriage was meant to lead to David's death. Saul could not do any harm to David openly so he decided to bless him in pretense so that he could be cursed. Any blessing that comes to you from the rejected Saul is a curse to you. You have to be careful what you call a blessing.

Watch out for any gift aimed at ensnaring you, it might be a gift to kill. This is the point that you must *break loose*.

The Bible records in the next verse that at the time Merab was to be given to David she was given to Adriel as wife. With this turn of events, David escaped the gift to kill.

Another Gift to Kill

Saul, realising he had lost his chance to give Merab to David as wife, he set up yet another trap for David to be killed by the Philistines.

"And Michal Saul's daughter loved David: and they told Saul and the thing pleased him. And Saul said, I will give him her, that she may be a snare to him, and that the hand of the philistines may be against him. Wherefore Saul said to David, thou shalt this day be my son in law in one of the twain" (1 Samuel 18:20-21).

Saul gave Michal to David not out of a pure heart but in order to ensnare him. He wanted the hands of the Philistines to prevail over him. Saul was determined to give one of his daughters to David as a snare. Be careful what you call a blessing. What you think is a blessing might be a trap to stop you from the real blessing.

Have you received a gift at some time in your life that has put you under a particular spell or bondage? I speak freedom into your life by the unction of the Holy Spirit!

There are some gifts that are irrevocably linked to demonic influence — gifts that allow the giver to monitor your life. Other gifts are used as instruments of oppression and suppression. You must be careful what you call a blessing.

Some naive people think that all gifts are given freely. You need to know that gifts given in deception are not free; you will have to pay for them in cash or in kind!

Some are still tied up to their past and different soul-ties because of the gifts they have received. Dubious people will want to bribe your intelligence and pay the price of stealing your integrity. They do this to prevent you from standing up for yourself. All that Saul was interested in doing was to stop David from reaching his ultimate breakthrough.

The Motive of the Giver

The motive of the giver determines the after effect of a gift on the receiver. Saul thought that the fastest way to kill an achiever is through blessing. The gift is not the problem but the motive of the giver is what matters.

If Saul blesses you, in his heart it is a curse. Every blessing of Saul–spirited people are snares and traps. I know there is somebody reading this book who has received an evil gift that is causing problems in the marriage. Some received gifts at birth that are causing problems today. Some people have been covenanted in exchange for a gift from the devil. You must check your life, search your roots and ask questions.

Your Destiny: The Price of Saul's Gifts

God has answered so many prayers in your life but because of the presence of gifts from Saul-spirited people your progress has been hindered. I know that I am speaking to someone right now who is already in the snare of the devil; it is not over yet! If you can make up your mind and be determined to break yourself loose from those bondages then you will be free in Jesus' name.

Be careful what you call a blessing. You should go home and search for what the enemy has set as a trap in your life. You have to think back and reflect on all the gifts you have received. Never host the gift from Saul; it is a trap to sift you.

"And the king said, Thus shall you say to David, the king desireth not any dowry, but an hundred foreskins of the Philistines, to be avenged of the kings enemies. But Saul thought to make David fall by the hand of the Philistines" (1 Samuel 18:25).

The king said he did not require any dowry and that David could have his daughter free of charge without any cost.

The cost of Saul's free gift is very expensive, nothing can pay for it other than a man's destiny. Saul was not interested in taking the money or material things, instead he was interested in the destiny of David.

For you to get to your ultimate breakthrough, you have to develop the spirit of discernment that will help you differentiate a snare from a blessing. Do not collect the gift of the enemy on the platform of blessings.

"And Saul spake to Jonathan his son, and to all his servants, that they should kill David" (1 Samuel 19:1).

He sent his servants to go and kill David; you have to be careful what you call a blessing and watch who speaks into your life. When you receive the gift of Saul, it puts a mark on you that will be indelible. This mark is a mark of the devil and everywhere you get to, you will be recognised as an evil prey in the hand of the wicked.

Be careful of Balak's gift. Balak gave a contract to the prophet to speak against the people of God. He wanted Balaam to curse the people of

God. Balaam was enticed by the gift and it took God to intervene his pursuit of it. Do not commit evil because of momentary compensation.

Elisha refused the gifts of Naaman because there was pride in Naaman's heart. Gehazi, however, ran after Naaman, lied to him and collected the gifts. This brought him under an automatic curse. Gehazi thought it was an opportunity to be enriched; he did not know that he was putting himself under a curse of leprosy, both him and his generation forever. You have to be careful what you call a blessing. When you receive a gift of deception, you will not harm only yourself, but also generations coming after you.

Some Truths About Gifts

♦ *A gift is a key to connection: "A man's gift maketh room for him, and bringeth him before great men." (Proverbs 18:16).*

♦ *Everybody is a friend of him that gives gifts: "...and every man is a friend to him that giveth gifts" (Proverbs 19:6b).*

♦ *You can silence an angry man with gifts: "A gift in secret pacifieth anger: and a reward in the bosom strong wrath" (Proverbs 21:14).*

♦   *A dishonest gift is a root of evil; never do evil because of momentary compensation:* "He that is greedy of gain troubleth his own house; but he that hateth gifts shall live" (Proverbs 15:27).

♦   *Watch out for gifts given to oppress; this is bribery:* "Surely oppression maketh a wise man mad, and a gift destroyeth the heart" (Ecclesiastes 7:7).

♦   *Take no gifts with strings attached:* "And thou shall take no gift, for the gift blindeth the wise, and perverteth the words of the righteous." (Exodus 23:8).

♦   *A false gift is an obstacle to breakthrough: Never promise anyone a gift you know you are not able to fulfill:* "Whoso boasteth himself of a false gift is like clouds and wind without rain." (Proverbs 25:14).

♦   *Never give or take bribes, it is a curse that blocks breakthrough:* "The king by judgment establisheth the land: but he that receiveth gifts overthroweth it." (Proverbs 29:4).

♦ ***Do not manipulate or be manipulated with gifts; such gifts may cause a drastic fall from grace to grass:*** *"A gift is a precious stone in the eyes of him that has it; withersoever it turneth, it prospereth: A wicked man taketh a gift out of the bossom to pervert the ways of judgment" (Proverbs 17:8,23).*

Perfect Blessing

"Every good gift and every perfect gift is from above, and cometh down from the father of lights, with whom is no variableness, neither shadow of turning" (James 1:17).

God is the only true Giver. His gifts have no sorrow in them. God has given us gifts especially the gift of eternal life and salvation: "For God so loved the world that he gave his only begotten son that whosoever believeth in Him should not perish but have everlasting life" (John 3:16). Every good gift from above is slated for the children of God. There is no enjoyable gift in the slave market of sin. Jesus is the perfect gift to the world.

Disappear From Evil Givers

When David knew that he was going to be killed, the bible says he departed that night. If God wants to bless you, do not relax in the house of someone that wants to kill you. Depart immediately and do not wait to collect the gift. Gifts are powerful, initiating, instigating and influential. Never sell your future for a gift of corruption.

I know you are going somewhere and you are going to experience your ultimate breakthrough. But be careful who seems to be helping you. Be on your guard against anything that can ensnare you. Your name is important so is your integrity.

WISDOM PRINCIPLES

Open praise and public ovation are dangerous especially when those who are losing their fame at the beginning of yours are there to witness your praise.

As you prepare to appear before the pharaoh of your vision, get ready to disappear before the Saul of your destiny.

Train your mind because chance favours the trained mind.

For every vision there is a pharaoh; for every journey to breakthrough there is a storm.

In every storm there is beauty and the beauty of your own storm is the wisdom you get from it.

God will rather replace man than allow His work to halt

It is possible for someone to be living under a glorious heaven and his life is not glorious.

*If you are not ready to celebrate others
you will not be celebrated.*

*Stop deliberating about others and
start celebrating them.*

*There is no indispensable mortal
before the immortal Creator.*

*There is a gift to heal and there is a gift to kill;
be careful what gift you receive.*

*David shared his past experiences with Saul
but he did not tell him the secret behind
the "sling shot".*

*Watch out for the gift aimed at ensnaring you,
it might be a gift to kill.*

*What you do when people are looking at you
is not the real assessment of
your Christian standard.*

*The motive of the giver determines
the effect of the gift on the receiver.*

*The cost of Saul's free gift is very expensive;
nothing can pay for it other than a man's destiny.*

*You should not rush out for the enjoyment
of a moment; pay the price of dignity.*

*Any blessing you get from a spiritual leper
is packaged in spiritual leprosy.*

Never sell your future for a gift of corruption.

ENEMY UNDER ARREST
(The Break-Down Zone)

When you succeed in scaling through the different "breaks" discussed in the previous chapters, it is time for you to cease from every struggle. At this crucial point in your journey, you will see the Lord break down every enemy in your life.

Even though Goliath was an intimidating giant, it is relatively easier to defeat Goliath than Saul. Goliath is a known enemy, but Saul an enemy disguised as a friend. Saul was making use of David to fight the Philistines, yet he did not want him to survive the battlefield. He did not fancy the idea that David will take over the throne from him. He was aware that the Lord had rejected him and that as he decreased, David was bound to increase.

After you escape from the traps of Saul, the Lord will bring you to the point where you can be at peace and watch Him fight for you. There are a series of battles at this break down zone but you do not need to do any fighting.

All the while you have been fighting and gaining experience. God's grace has been sufficient for you. But at the break down zone, the Lord does not need your experience; He takes over the battle and does the fighting.

Knowing that this is the last junction before you enter your winning zone, the enemy will mobilise his strongest troops to attack you. This is the "break down" point (either you break down or the enemy breaks down). If you can pass this mile, the battle will be all over; you will move unhindered into your ultimate break-through.

The enemy will assume that you are the same person, forgetting that there is a greater God living in you who is mightier than the mightiest authority. This leaves an impact and something begins to happen on the outside and what happens on the outside has a direct negative impact on the enemy. At this point, the Lord will break down the enemy completely.

No weapon fashioned against you will prosper at the break down zone. You would not have to struggle or fight. You will only need to stand by and watch God in action. The Scriptures declare, "Surely they shall gather but not by me, whosoever shall gather together against you shall fall for your sake." When God is fighting your battle, all your enemies are subdued under your feet.

At the break down zone, all your enemies are like grass under your feet. God will arrest all your adversaries because any tongue that rises against you in judgment shall be condemned. When they fashion any weapon against you it will not prosper. Anyone that is trying is just wasting time because God is fighting on your behalf.

There are some emissaries that God will arrest for you. Let us identify some of them in the following sections.

The Sennacheribs

The Sennacheribs are enemies that aim to attack you at this particular phase in your life. They have no other aim than to destroy you. This is the first kind of enemy that the Lord will deal with.

In *2 Chronicles 32*, Sennacherib and his troops besieged the people of God and set a certain time to destroy them. In the same manner, the devil will sometimes wait for a time that his deadly attacks can have the most devastating effect.

For instance, a woman may have a smooth pregnancy only to meet the adversary waiting for her at the point of delivery. A spinster may be facing Sennacheribs at the point of getting married; they might have said, "We will not allow her to get married until she is fifty"!

Sennacheribs are the spirits or people who do not want you to get any certificate out of your university; forces that do not want you to move up to a new level. These are spirits who allow you to get engaged for a few months only to disrupt the relationship before the wedding day. These are the Sennacheribs at work. They want you to keep busy until their plan to attack you is suddenly unleashed.

You do not need to be afraid or frustrated. God will put the enemy under arrest in your life. They have decided to fight you for no just reason. This is why God has declared the battle to be His and not yours.

The Pharaohs

These are the taskmasters who always want to use the best in you for their own selfish ends and to your detriment. Pharaoh did not want to release the children of Israel. God, therefore, arose on their behalf and brought them out on eagles' wings.

God demonstrated the deliverance process to Moses with the burning bush. The bush was burning but was not consumed. This signified that things might be hot and uneasy now, but the fire will have a soothing and beautifying effect at the end. It will not ultimately destroy you. After you have been tried, you will come forth as pure gold. Every fire that you are going through is not to kill or consume you but to beautify you and make you come forth as pure gold. Remember, there is no gain without pain.

You have been dealing with the Eliabs, Goliaths, Jonadabs and Sauls; it is time to stop *fighting* and start *watching*. Israel got to their break down zone and Pharaoh, who did not want them to go, had no choice but to order their release. The angel of the Lord killed all the Egyptian firstborn because God was fighting the battle for Israel.

Allow God to do the fighting for you. Whoever wants to loot what you worked for will pay dearly for it. We are the spiritual Israelites and nobody can squander what we laboured for.

This is the time that God will receive for you what belongs to you. If God determines that all your enemies will kill themselves, it shall be so. The enemies are under arrest and the pharaoh of your life is destroyed (Exodus 14:21-30). The same God who did it then can do it again.

The Amonites, Moabites and the People of Mount Seir

These are executive conspirators. Even though they are not friends with each other, they have found a common cause to be united — they do not want you to get to the next level of your breakthrough. They have decided to come together because they are not interested in your destiny and progress. They want to hinder your progress at all cost. However, at this break down zone, God will make an open show of them.

"It came to pass after this also, that the children of Moab, and the children of Ammon, and with them other beside the Ammonites, came against Jehoshaphat to battle. Then there came some that

told Jehoshaphat, saying, There cometh a great multitude against thee from beyond the sea on this side Syria; and, behold, they be in Haza-zon-tamar, which is Engedi. And Jehoshaphat feared, and set himself to seek the Lord, and proclaimed a fast throughout all Judah. And Judah gathered themselves together, to ask help of the Lord: even out of all the cities of Judah they came to seek the Lord. And Jehoshaphat stood in the congregation of Judah and Jerusalem, in the house of the Lord before the new court, And said, O Lord God of our fathers, art not thou God in heaven? And in thine hand is there not power and might, so that none is able to withstand thee?" (2 Chronicles 20:1-6).

Do not be afraid of what the enemy can do. All you need to do is get closer to God and contact the master of your life through the control tower of prayer. If some unusual things come to disturb you, ascend to the control tower; keep on going and do not be afraid. God, who is an unusual God, will use unusual means to remove the unusual problem.

Let us consider a few lessons from how God fought for Israel in this battle before examining David's experience at this stage.

Get Yourself Ready

"And all Judah stood before the Lord, with their little ones, their wives and their children." (2 Chronicles 20:13).

They brought their children as well, because they were ready for a great time in God's presence. They were all fasting and waiting on God. Everyone came "in the midst of the congregation" and gave themselves totally to seek the face of God. They did not come as spectators but as active participators.

This is time that God wants us to grow "in the midst of the congregation" and be active in the house of God. Do not be afraid of the great multitude that is against you for the battle is not yours but the Lord's.

You Do Not Need to Fight

"Be not dismayed by reason of this great multitude; for the battle is not yours but God's:... ye shall not need to fight in this battle: set yourselves, stand ye still and see the salvation of the Lord with you" (2 Chronicles 20:15b-17).

At the break down zone, you do not need to do any fighting; you should not bother yourself or

Heavenly Ambushments

When God fights for you, it will be evident that He is the One in battle.

"And when they began to sing and to praise, the Lord set ambushments against the children of Ammon, Moab and Mount Seir, which were come against Judah: and they were smitten" (2 Chronicles 20:22).

The Lord set an ambushment on the enemy. An ambushment on the wicked makes sure that they lose the battle whichever way they turn.

Three sets of people came together to fight the children of God but the Lord ensured that the Ammonites and the Moabites fought each other. First, they made an utter end of mount Seir and later began to fight and kill themselves. When God fights for you, people who have planned to kill you will turn against each other.

"For the children of Ammon and Moab stood up against the inhabitants of mount Seir, utterly to slay and destroy them: and when they had made an end of the inhabitants of Seir, every one helped to destroy another" (2 Chronicles 20:23).

The Great Escape

"And David fled, and escaped, and came to Samuel to Ramah, and told him all that Saul had done to him. And he and Samuel went and dwelt in Naioth." (1 Samuel 19:18).

At David's break down zone, it was necessary for him to hide from Saul. There are times you need to hide yourself and refuse to show up. If you show up at the wrong time you will expose yourself to great danger. David hid from Saul and the people with him provided adequate protection. However, news came to Saul about the location of David and he came to capture David there.

David's wise reaction was to run away. There are times you need to run from the Saul of your destiny. If the Saul of your destiny will die, it will not be through your own hands but through the hands of God.

The Prophecy of the Emissary

"So David fled and escaped, and came to Samuel to Ramah, and told him all that Saul had done to him. And he and Samuel went and dwelt in Naioth. And it was told Saul, saying, Behold David is at Naioth in Ramah. And Saul sent

*messengers to take David: and when they saw
the company of the prophets prophesying, and
Samuel standing as appointed over them, the
Spirit of God was upon all the messengers of
Saul, and they also prophesied. And when it was
told Saul, he sent other messengers, and they
prophesied likewise. And Saul sent messengers
again the third time, and they prophesied also.
Then went he to Ramah, and came to a great wall
that is in Sechu: and he asked and said, Where
are Samuel and David? And one said, Behold,
they be at Naoith in Ramah. And he went thither
to Naioth in Ramah. And the Spirit of God was
upon him also, and he went on, and prophesied,
until he came to Naioth in Ramah. And he
stripped off his clothes also, and prophesied
before Samuel in like manner, and laid down
naked all that day and all that night. Wherefore
they say, Is Saul also among the prophets?" (1
Samuel 19:18-24).*

David fled from the palace and ran to Samuel.
He went to the house of God to meet the prophet.
You should make sure you share your situations
with the right people and not just anybody.

When Saul heard that David was with Samuel,
he ordered that both Samuel and David should
be killed. However, when the emissary came
over to where Samuel and David were, they

began to prophesy; they delivered messages that Saul did not give them. The Spirit of God came on them and their assignment was nullified. They started to prophesy about David's ultimate breakthrough—the very thing Saul did not want to hear. God knows how to get your evil emissaries to speak about your greatness.

The Open Shame of Saul

When Saul heard about the incidence, he sent some other messengers more powerful than the first. On getting to Naioth, they also prophesied. A third set of messengers also came and prophesied as well.

After all of these attempts to capture David had failed, amazingly, Saul decided to go himself! The truth is, Saul will go to any length to eliminate you; but because God is fighting on your behalf, you do not need to lift a finger. God knows what to do to arrest your enemies!

Saul arose and went to Ramah. He asked for where to get both Samuel and David. On the way to the prophet's house, the Spirit of God that had departed from Saul in a long time came back on him just to confirm David's reign!

It does not matter how wicked your Saul is, at the break down zone they will pronounce your elevation. The enemy will begin to propagate the gospel of your success. The people Saul sent earlier did not prophesy until they got to the place where David and Samuel were but the Lord caused Saul to prophesy around the city. The Lord just wanted to make an open show of the bitter king. He started to speak well about David and reverse all the curses he had spoken against him. Every negative word became positive.

When people saw king Saul, they were surprised to hear what he was prophesying because they all knew he wanted to kill David.

When he got to where David was, instead of just prophesying like the other servants, the Lord made sure he ridiculed himself by stripping naked as he prophesied. The Lord wanted to make an open show of him.

Before he could qualify to speak to David he had to report to him naked. He was naked on the ground all day long. He could not even stand up or sit sown. He laid helpless on the ground for a very long time.

When God strips your enemies naked before you, all of their secret agendas will be uncovered. Nothing will remain hidden anymore. You would not need to raise a finger against them because God is vindicating you at the break down zone. The news spread round Israel and it became a saying that "Is Saul also among the prophets?"

Whatever it costs you, make sure you enter the break down zone. Overcome your Eliabs and Goliaths; secure divine friendships with your Jonathans; avoid the entrapments of deceptive gifts and you will experience stress-free, pain-free victories as the Lord fights all your battles for you.

WISDOM PRINCIPLES

Even though Goliath was an intimidating giant, it is relatively easier to defeat Goliath than Saul. Goliath is a known enemy, but Saul an enemy disguised as a friend.

When David rises, Saul must fall. The beginning of your rising marks the beginning of your enemy's fall.

Whatever has a direct positive impact on you will have a direct negative impact on your enemies.

The original plan of God is to take you to the position of excellence. Why settle for less?

The plans of the wicked to destroy you is a timed bomb that will blow up in their face.

The fire that has a soothing and beautifying effect on you will produce a destructive effect on the enemy.

There is no gain without a pain;
there is no glory without a story.

God is an unusual God;
He can use unusual means to remove
unusual problems.

When the wicked conspire against you,
it will backfire with a devastating effect.

God is not moved by spectators
but by participators.

Your confirmation and assessment
does not come from man but from God.

The accumulation of your experience
is the qualification for a greater gain.

Your back will never be on the ground,
when God is backing you.

The authority of the prophetic sanction
over you is your certificate for prosperity.

The stronghold is the control tower where
you can get hold of power to control.

Those who thought to turn you naked will
report themselves naked to talk to you.

Those who hate you
will announce your arrival.

The point of Break Down is when God breaks
all your enemies down without consulting you.

MILE SIX

ENTERING THE WINNING ZONE
(The Break-Even Zone)

Y ou have passed through different stages on the way to your ultimate breakthrough. You have learnt what to do at the beginning of success, how to bring down the Goliath of your life, how to engage in friendship by divine connection, how to discern the right and wrong gift, how God intends to put the enemy under arrest. Now, we need to know what to do when entering the next break—the winning zone.

The Break-Even Point

After the Lord arrests your adversaries and makes an open show of them, He will usher you into your winning zone. This is the point where you experience success.

For the most part, you have been in obscurity between the beginning of your success and the winning zone. However, at the winning zone, your breakthrough becomes visible. At the winning zone it is hard to fail.

Even you are surprised because the same things you have been doing before with little results now yields greater returns. When you arrive at your winning zone, you will begin to possess things easily and without stress.

God allowed you to go through all the previous "breaks" so that you will develop vital experience for the future. The wisdom you gained in past confrontations will become useful during future battles. You will also be able to share your experience with others in the same predicament. This is the point that you break-even.

Sample Success

"And it came to pass after this, that David enquired of the Lord, saying, Shall I go up into any of the cities of Judah? And the Lord said unto him, Go up. And David said, Whither shall I go up? And he said, Unto Hebron. So David

went up thither, and his two wives also, Ahinoam the Jezreelitess, and Abigail Naban's wife the Carmelite. And his men that were with him did David bring up, everyman with his household; and they dwelt in the cities of Hebron. And the men of Judah came, and there they anointed David king over the house of Judah. And they told David, saying, that the men of Jabesh-gilead were they that buried Saul." (2 Samuel 2:1-4).

In this scripture, it was confirmed that Saul had died and been buried. The natural consequence of this was that people came to David and anointed him king. God's pronouncements over David began to find fulfillment as he was made king over the tribe of Judah (even though the promise was to make him king over the tribes of Israel).

When David was made king at Hebron, he entered his winning zone. The word of the Lord had not come to pass in full but he was on the way to experiencing its full manifestation. Although he was king over two tribes, he was still going to be king over twelve. His kingship over two tribes was an introduction to the ultimate breakthrough.

So, when you get to your winning zone, the first thing that comes into your life is sample success. The sample success is a standing proof that you can get the real thing.

What to do at the Winning Zone

Understand that your first entrance into the winning zone is just the beginning of your break-through; it will usher you to the realm of great success. But there are still some things that God will want you to do.

You must be careful of "the son of a stranger the Amalekite". Be on your guard against tale-bearers who want to send you backwards to previous breaking points. If you dance to their tune and listen to their gossip, God will cease to fight for you. Be watchful, therefore, for anything that wants to make you to fail. Do not be merciful to such distracting agents.

It is better not to experience success at all than for you to experience it and go backwards. Be careful of the Amalekite that will drag you back.

"Then said Saul unto his armourbearer, Draw thy sword and thrust me through therewith; lest these uncircumcised come and thrust me through, and abuse me. But his armourbearer would not; for he was sore afraid. Therefore Saul took a sword, and fell upon it. And when his armourbearer saw that Saul was dead, he fell

likewise upon his sword, and died with him. So Saul died, and his three sons, and his armour-bearer, and all his men that same day together" (1 Samuel 31:4).

When God is fighting on your behalf, do not interfere with your own knowledge and presumptions. Things may not be exactly the way you want them to be, but it is only a matter of time—you will get to your destination.

When you enter your winning zone, you do not need to do anything about those who oppose you. Those who have sought to kill you will turn against themselves. You will not need to bother yourself about them anymore; you have entered your winning zone.

A single day is enough to cancel the pain you are going through today. I have news for you: that "single day" can be today. God will cancel all your pain in Jesus' name.

"And it came even to pass on the third day, that, behold, a man came out of the camp from Saul with his clothes rent, and earth upon his head: and so it was, when he came to David, that he fell to the earth, and did obeisance. And David said unto him, from whence cometh thou? And he said unto him, Out of the camp of Israel am I escaped" (2 Samuel 1:2).

If nobody seems to care about you today, wait until your prosperity begins to show forth! Everyone will want to be your friend! Some who have heard of the exploits happening in your life will write you. Some will even tell you they are writing by the instruction of God! People will come to you with different lies in order to seek your favour.

When such people approach you, like the Amalekite that came to David, test them out with one or two questions. If they have come with deceit, they will become nervous and will commit themselves. This is a necessary test you must carry out on people, strangers in particular, when you enter your winning zone.

Struggle-Free Zone

When you begin to enter your winning zone, things work for you; you are highly favoured by God and people; things you have struggled for will come to you quite easily; everything is ordered by God; goodness and mercy follows you all the days of your life. You would not fear what people say because your winning zone is a struggle-free zone. If you tried to arrive before your arrival time, little things would be difficult and you will always have to please everybody.

False Evidences of the Amalekites

The Amalekite that came to David was formerly in the camp of Saul but when he realised that Saul had lost, he decided to come to the camp of David and pretend as a friend.

"And David said unto him, How went the matter, I pray thee, tell me. And he answered, That the people are fled from the battle, and many of the people are fallen and dead; and Saul and Jonathan his son are dead also" (2 Samuel 1:4).

This Amalekite was the first to announce the death of Saul and Jonathan. At first hearing, it sounded like a good report. However, at the winning zone, you must be sensitive to the Holy Spirit. Develop the discernment of spirit to know the motive behind people's words and actions.

David obviously learnt from this experience when he said in the Psalms that God should shut the door of his mouth when an evil man is before him. He was referring to people who come with an Amalekite spirit.

"And David said unto the young man that told him, How knowest thou that Saul and Jonathan his son be dead?" (2 Samuel 1:5).

The Amalekite will always claim that they "happened by chance". Do not fall for their vices. They are experts in sowing discords amongst brethren. It is dangerous to listen to gossip and slander. The fact that you do not allow some people entry into your life does not mean that you hate them. You can always help them by your responses. The Amalekites want to force you to make unnecessary promises so that they can hold you by your words.

"And the young man said, As I happened by chance upon mount Gilboa, behold Saul leaned upon his spear; and, lo, the chariots and horsemen followed hard after him. And when he looked behind him, he saw me, and called unto me. And I answered, Here am I. And he said unto me, Who art thou? And I answered him, I am an Amalikite. And he said unto me again, Stand I pray thee, upon me, and slay me: for anguish is come upon me, because my life is yet whole in me" (2 Samuel 1:6,7).

This man told a lie in attempt to seek favour from the person he once persecuted. He told a lie in order to decamp. It was not him that killed Saul but Saul killed himself with the sword. Amalekites are professional liars; they tell so many lies that you will feel their words are true.

You have to learn how to discern people after the spirit and not after the flesh.

Presentation of Evidences

"So I stood upon him, and slew him, because I was sure that he could not live after that he was fallen: and I took the crown that was upon his head, and the bracelet that was on his arm, and have brought them hither unto my lord" (2 Samuel 1:10).

He presented physical evidences to support his lies. He was not even at the scene of the incidence but he had physical proofs for his lies! When an Amalekite talks, be sure you listen with your inner ears too!

That a person tells you so much about a situation and even presents evidences does not mean the truth is spoken. Beware of those, in particular, who want to destroy others to gain favour with you. Such people only want to enter your vehicle of destiny and accompany your entourage into the ultimate breakthrough zone. You must be careful.

Clear off the Stranger!

Do not allow Amalekites to speak for too long in your presence. They can sow dangerous seeds in your spirit and hinder your progress. If you allow them, you may remain at the entry zone without entering your ultimate breakthrough. For you to enter your ultimate breakthrough you have to first deal with the Amalekites.

Amalekites may represent evil thoughts in your mind or people who you meet. As you enter your winning zone, you must clear off the dirt from your way. A talebearer is a dangerous person. The words of a talebearer are like deep wounds that go into the innermost part of the belly. They will always remain there to torment you unless you get rid of them.

The preacher in Ecclesiastes says that you must not even be a friend to a talebearer; you should run away from a talebearer. Amalekites are talebearers and they will always find their way to you. The moment you listen to them long enough to gather accurate information, let the sword of righteousness fall back on their heads.

"And David said unto the young man that told him, Whence are thou? And he answered I am a son of a stranger the Amalekite" (2 Samuel 1:13).

Be careful for "the son of a stranger the Amalekite". Such strangers, with no traceable background, are dangerous. You cannot afford to affiliate closely with someone who has no credible history. It does not matter how interesting their story sounds, if it cannot be verified, let your alert buttons stay on.

Never Kill the Lord's Anointed

"And David said, How wast thou not afraid to stretch forth thine hand to destroy the Lord's anointed?" (2 Samuel 1:14).

The mistake of this stranger was that he did not know that David feared God. He assumed wrongly that David would rejoice with him and give him a reward. His judgment and calculation were based on worldly thinking. He did not realise that David had the mind of God.

David did not consider Saul an enemy; he saw him as the anointed of God. The Amalekite did not know that David had twice rejected the opportunity to kill Saul. His miscalculation cost him his life.

When you get to your winning zone, do not attempt to make everybody your friend, especially strange Amalekites. Be careful not to take lightly those things that you did not take for granted before your elevation.

Also, be sensitive about people who would attempt to relate with you just because you have entered your winning zone (particularly those who once despised you).

The End of the Amalekite

"And David called one of the young men, and said, Go near and fall upon him. And he smote him that he died. And David said unto him, Thy blood be upon thy head; for thy mouth hath testified against thee, saying, I have slain the Lord's anointed" (2 Samuel 1:15,16).

God hates the Amalekites. He hates slander and those who sow discord among the brethren. The end of every Amalekite thought in you should be "death". Do not allow such vain imagination to dwell in you. The sooner you deal with it the better.

Also deal with every manipulative relationship; any stranger that wants to gain illegal access into your life. Anything not ordained of God should be terminated.

Keep on Going!

Always inquire of the Lord before you make decisions. Refuse to be carried away by people who applaud you for little achievements. Such ovation can break your focus on the ultimate breakthrough. Keep on moving forward and do not celebrate success for too long. You still have a lot of things to achieve in life.

David inquired of the Lord before he laid his hands on anything. He asked God whether he should go to the cities of Judah and the Lord said, "Go up". (The influence of the Amalekite would have brought David *down* but God wanted him to go *up*). When you make a habit of inquiring from God about everything, you will constantly hear Him tell you, "Go up".

David's desire was not to confront problems or mountains; he asked to go to the cities of Judah, that is, the cities of "praise". This teaches us to always ascend to God in worship and praise. As you praise God, He will continue to raise you up. The person that cannot praise will not be raised. Praise is your license to elevation.

Keep on going up. Do not rest with the miracles of yesterday. "Go up" and enter the city of praise.

Do Not Import Foreign Ideas

As you enter your winning zone, do not import foreign ideas. Importation of foreign ideas at this stage of your journey is a master key to a landslide failure. David trained and made use of his own men—people that were with him from the beginning. He did not appoint men from outside but grew leaders from his own camp. It is important you groom your own leaders. You are a good leader when people no longer need you before they can function. Deposit yourself in others and they will carry on the good work you started.

David was a wonderful warrior and he raised a great army for God. What kind of army are you building? Make sure you build your people up with you and together you will bring glory to the kingdom of God.

Do not allow the satisfaction of your first success to divert you from God's presence. You have not attained your ultimate yet; there is still a long way to go. What you have achieved now is not the pinnacle of success. Move on towards your next level of success.

At your winning zone...

Let us summarise the things you need to do at your winning zone (and remember you are just a step to your ultimate breakthrough).

♦ Always inquire of the Lord before taking any step (Proverbs 3:5,6)

♦ Let your decisions be Theo-centric (that is, God-centered) and not egocentric (that is, self-centered). Egocentricity is the master key to a landslide failure. This is when you ask God to step aside for you to act.

♦ Do not brag about the things of this world. Whatever the amount of investment you have, let nothing break your relationship with God.

♦ Lay your treasure in heaven where there is no decay or loss. (Matthew 6:19).

♦ Do not let the breeze of success make you forget the toil of breakthrough. When enjoyment comes into your life, do not forget your source. Be careful of your "valley experience".

♦ Remember God at the cool time of your life.

WISDOM PRINCIPLES

*No gossip can stand in the way
of a true worshipper.*

*The sample success you experience is a
standing proof that you can get the real thing.*

*Success not experienced is better than
success that is followed by failure.*

Your winning zone is struggle-free zone.

*Do not give attention to an "Amalekite";
they are experts in sowing discord
among the brethren.*

*Do not allow just anyone into your life.
The fact that you refuse some people entry into your
life does not mean that you hate them.*

*The demotion the wicked thought for you
automatically propels you to your promotion.*

Do not celebrate success for too long.
You still have many things to achieve.

A man who is busy begging God
does not beg men. When you pray to God,
you don't pray to men.

Praise is your license to go up
to another level of breakthrough

Do not import foreign ideas.
Importation of foreign ideas is a master key
to a landside failure.

You are a good leader when people no longer
need you before they can function.

Do not allow the satisfaction of success carry you
away from God's presence.

Never base life decisions
on the advice of a stranger.

Do not let the breeze of success make you forget the
toil of breakthrough.

Remember God at the cool time of your life.

ASENDING THE
THRONE OF DESTINY
(The Ultimate Breakthrough Zone)

At last! Your destination is in view. Your moment of ultimate breakthrough is round the corner. You are about to leave the position of *not enough* and *just enough* and are getting ready to move to the realm of *more than enough!* This is the peak of success; the destination of your journey.

You have left the preliminary breakthrough level;

You have left the Break Out level

You have left the Break Away level

You have left the Break In level

You have left the Break Off level

You have left the Break Loose level

You have left the Break Down level

You are presently on the Break Even level.

You now need to move to the "Ultimate Breakthrough" level.

Wait for the Moment

This is the moment you have been waiting for. For everyone and every problem in life, there is a *moment* you have been waiting for; the reason why you kept on going against the odds.

When a woman enters into her contraction period, she bears all the pain because there is a moment she is waiting for. This is the moment of joy that causes all pain to disappear. At your moment of ultimate breakthrough you no longer fear anything. Instead, things begin to fear you.

At the ultimate point, doors and ways begin to open without the lifting of a finger; people turn to you and say that you have arrived.

At the moment of ultimate breakthrough, people see you as an expert in everything you do, this is not because you have just learnt any new thing but because you are at the fullness of time.

We have examined the life of David as he travelled from his preliminary breakthrough towards his ultimate breakthrough. He has been termed "a man after God's heart" because he knew how to follow God; he knew the character and principles of God. God is not a respecter of persons but of principles. You must understand the principles of God.

In the earlier chapter, we discussed that David was crowned king in Hebron over two tribes but that was not the God's ultimate for him. God wanted him to be king over all the tribes of Israel.

"Then came all the tribes of Israel to David unto Hebron, and spake, saying, Behold, we are thy bone and thy flesh. Also in time past, when Saul was king over us, thou wast he that leddest out and broughtest in Israel: and the Lord said to thee, thou shalt feed my people Israel, and thou shalt be a captain over Israel. So all the elders of Israel came to the king to Hebron; and king David made a league with them in Hebron before the Lord: and they anointed David king over Israel. David was thirty years when he began to reign, and he reigned forty years. In Hebron he reigned over Judah seven years and six months: and in Jerusalem he reigned thirty and three years over all Israel and Judah." (2 Samuel 5:1-5).

Be faithful to God as you pass through various ordeals on the way to your ultimate breakthrough. You cannot escape any of the "breaks" that precede this level. As we noted earlier, you gain experience by going through these phases. Attaining the height of success is not as important as acquiring the type of character (from experience) that will sustain you there.

The Reward of Selfless Service

When the people came to David, he was king over only two tribes but they knew that he should be king over all the tribes of Israel. People who know your worth cannot ascribe it to you especially when they are under bad leadership. Saul was the controlling power but there were people who knew what God had said about David and they were ready to pursue it.

The people came and confessed, "We are your bone and your flesh." In other words, they were saying, "We are your strength and your weaknesses; we are your assets and we are your liabilities; we know that God has ordained you to take care of us; you have been the one solving the problems in the land." This implies that throughout the time of David's service, the people were taking cognizance of his selfless efforts and they knew it was time for his lifting.

Whatever service you are offering to others, do not think that it is in vain or that God will not reward you. The bible gives this encouragement: *"And let us not be weary in well doing; for in due season we shall reap, if we faint not." (Galatians 6:9).*

The condition for reaping the harvest here is to "faint not." If you do not faint, your adversary will faint instead. If you do not give up, the enemy will give up at last.

They all came together and anointed David as king over all the twelve tribes of Israel because this was his ultimate breakthrough.

When you get to your moment of ultimate breakthrough, things begin to work for you. Favour comes into your life in an extraordinary way. People begin to follow your leadership. Kings shall come to the brightness of your shining. At this point in your life, you will arise and shine because your light has come and the glory of God is risen upon you (Isaiah 60:1).

Hear the word of King David at the height of his success:

"Thou hast delivered me from the strivings of the people; and thou hast made me the head of the

heathen: a people whom I have not known shall serve me. As soon as they hear of me, they shall obey me: the strangers shall submit themselves unto me." (Psalm 18:43-44)

At the ultimate breakthrough point, even the unbelievers will experience the breeze of your success because you will become a light bearer.

"And the gentiles shall come to thy light, and the kings to the brightness of your rising" (Isaiah 60:3).

At your ultimate breakthrough zone, your crown attracts favour and blessings begin to roll in without the lifting of a finger.

"And the sons of strangers shall build up thy wall, and their kings shall minister unto thee; for in my wrath I smote thee, but in my favour have I had mercy on thee. Therefore thy gates shall be open continually; they shall not be shut day nor night; that men may bring unto thee the forces of the gentiles, and that their kings may be brought" (Isaiah 60:10,11).

At your ultimate breakthrough zone, material provisions flow into you from every angle, especially, from places you did not expect.

"Thou shalt also suck the milk of the Gentiles, and shalt suck the breast of kings: and thou shalt know that I the Lord am thy Saviour and Redeemer, the mighty One of Jacob" (Isaiah 60:16).

You will enjoy a landslide victory at this ultimate realm; you would have no more wars to fight.

"Violence shall no more be heard in thy land, wasting nor destruction within thy borders; but thou shalt call thy walls Salvation, and thy gates Praise." (Isaiah 60:18).

At the ultimate, there is everlasting joy and no more sorrow for you.

"Thy sun shall no more go down; neither shall thy moon withdraw itself: for the Lord shall be thine everlasting light, and the days of thy mourning shall be ended" (Isaiah 60:20).

At the ultimate breakthrough zone, you will experience great revival of righteousness, peace and joy in the Holy Ghost among your people.

"Thy people also shall be all righteous: they shall inherit the land forever, the branch of my planting, the works of my hands, that I may be glorified" (Isaiah 60:21).

At the ultimate, you will be fruitful, multiply, replenish the earth, subdue it and possess your dominion mandate. Your ultimate breakthrough will overflow into lives around you and into generations after you. Even the least among your offspring shall be called "great".

"A little one shall become a thousand, and a small one a strong nation: I the Lord will hasten it in his time" (Isaiah 60:22).

Note something very important here. When David stepped into his ultimate breakthrough zone, he did not loose his guard. He was sensitive to divine direction and not carried away by momentary gratification. He fought and took over the stronghold of Zion. While people were busy dancing round the city, David was busy fortifying and preserving the stronghold for lasting glorification.

Before you relax, make sure you see the ultimate end of the adversaries of your destiny. Remember, possibilities and eventualities are powerful competitors on the field of absolute success. Be sure you prepare against any surprise attacks by destroying the enemies' future strategies through prayer warfare.

When you enter into your ultimate breakthrough, do not rush out of the "hold;"

keep living there.   Develop a life of prayer because you need more strength in God. Even success has its own accompanying problems. In other words, do what David did.

Go Into the Fort

"So David dwelt in the fort, and called it the city of David. And David built round about from Millo and inward." (2 Samuel 5:9).

David knew it was not the time for him to relax. He, therefore, remained in the fort—the place of prayer. He dwelt in the fort because he was a warrior and he was used to fighting. The bible says, *"woe unto them that are at ease in Zion" (Amos 6:1).* When God lifts you up, you should not relax.   Arriving at the top of the mountain is not the end of the road because to descend is much easier.

Be careful for the valley experience. It is very easy to fall when you are at the top. When you were still climbing you put in much effort not to fall. The same effort is needed at the top.

People tend to draw closer to God when there is a situation to pray about but when everything becomes rosy, they tend to forget God. Do not leave the fort. When you perceive that God has raised you and established your destiny, you must go into the fort. It is not the time to relax.

"And David perceived that the Lord had established him king over Israel, and that he had exalted his kingdom for his people Israel's sake" (2 Samuel 5:12).

When God is at work in your life, you will know. It is He that establishes kingdoms, homes, matrimonies, businesses and destinies. If God is with you, nobody can be against you. You must perceive that the Lord is with you.

David perceived that the Lord was with him and he entered into his ultimate breakthrough. When God is with you, there will be a transition from grass to grace.

Make sure, at this stage, you remain in the fort and never lose your praying power. God is interested in your humility and consistency in serving Him. David feared the Lord with all his heart. When you fear the Lord you will fulfill destiny before you die.

Make sure God takes the preeminence in everything you do. He allowed you to be broken so that you can become a master at mending lives. Personal testimony is a master key to releasing faith in others. Remember God at the cool of the day. Let your lifestyle be a testimony to people around you.

Divine Reinforcement

"But when the philistines heard that they had anointed David king over Israel, and the Philistines came up to seek David; and David heard of it, and went to the hold." (2 Samuel 5:17).

When the enemy hears about the success of God in your life, they will be surprised and they will come looking for you. Do not be afraid at the appearance of the Philistines. All you need to do is get into your hold, which is Jesus. Those who hate you will be thrown into confusion when they recognise that God is with you.

This is the ultimate zone. It is time for you to maintain and retain your success. When the Philistines heard that David had been made king, they were troubled. When, however, David heard that the Philistines knew he was king, he was not troubled; he went into the hold. He went into his place of power and authority. Immediately you enter into your success, do not lose your guard. You should always make sure you reinforce yourself in the hold.

Heavenly Connections

"The Philistines also came and spread themselves in the valley of Rephaim. And David enquired of the Lord, saying, Shall I go up to the Philistines? Wilt thou deliver them into mine hand? And the Lord said unto David, Go up; for I will doubtless deliver the Philistines into thine hand" (2 Samuel 5:18,19).

David enquired of the Lord how to confront the Philistines. He was able to enquire of the Lord because he was positioned in the place of prayer. Do not lose your guard. Tighten up the more and be on fighting mode. Do not wait for the ovation of men; go into the hold.

At your ultimate, make sure you always enquire of the Lord, do not think you know everything. For you to enjoy your continuous progress, you need to maintain your personal relationship with God. Remain connected to heaven at all times; your connection to heaven is the main determinant of your progression in life.

The Ultimate Moment

"And David came to Baal-perazim, and David smote them there, and said, The Lord hath broken forth upon mine enemies before me, as the breach

of waters. Therefore he called the name of that place Baal-perazim." (2 Samuel 5:20).

You must get to Baal-perazim, which means, "Possessor of the Breaches". This is the place where you possess all your possessions; the place where you close the gap and displace the enemy completely; the place where the enemy has no entrance into your life; the place where the enemy knows nothing about you anymore neither can he handle your breakthrough anymore. No matter what they knew about you, God will cause a permanent damage in their mind that will make them forget what they had planned to do. You have reached your Baal-perazim where there is total elimination of the Philistines. This was the place of David's landslide victory.

Evil Images

"And there they left their images, and David and his men burned them. And the Philistines came up yet again, and spread themselves in the valley of Rephaim." (2 Samuel 5:21,22).

When God hands over the enemy to you, the first thing you see is their images of worship. Some people have left your life but they still left their images. The oppressor is gone but the oppression is still there. The images are still there; oppression is more dangerous than the oppressor because after the oppressor is gone, the oppression remains.

The Philistines are very dangerous; you need to go into the hold again. Do not let your title rob you of your entitlement before the Lord. Your title has no rating before God; it is only recognised by men. The only title God recognises is His covenant-keeping Son, Jesus Christ.

Do Not Predict God

"And when David enquired of the Lord, He said, thou shalt not go up, but fetch a compass behind them, and come upon them over against the mulberry trees. And let it be, when thou hearest the sound of a going in the top of the mulberry trees, that then thou shalt bestir thyself: for then shalt the Lord go out before thee to smite the host of the Philistines." (2 Samuel 5:23,24).

In spite of the fact that the Philistines had been defeated by David, they once again came to attack him. David went up to enquire of the Lord again, and the Lord said he should not go up to the Philistines as usual. Instead, God gave David another strategy with which to defeat the Philistines. This shows the importance of inquiring from God always.

Never predict God. Always wait on Him for direction before any venture. Yesterday's strategy is too old for today's battle. God may have given you success in business last year, but now that you want to start another one, you still need to ask God for direction. Make sure you speak to God so that He can give you fresh orders. God is a mighty warrior and a strategic fighter.

"And David did so as the Lord had commanded him; and smote the Philistine from Gilboa until thou come to Gazer." (2 Samuel 5:25).

You must do whatever God asks you to do. Remember, when you were struggling, you received instructions from God. Now that your breakthrough has come, do not stop receiving instructions from Him. People will suggest different ideas to you. Be careful not to take opinions or advices that will make God remove His hands from your life.

Joseph's Experience

There are more things to learn about ultimate breakthroughs from the experiences of Joseph.

"And Pharaoh said unto Joseph, for has much as God has shewed thee all these, there is none so discreet and wise as thou hath: Thou shalt be

over my house and according unto thy word shall all my people be ruled: only in throne will I be greater than thou" (Genesis 41:39,40).

When Joseph interpreted Pharaoh's dream, he entered into his moment of ultimate breakthrough. God caused the king of Egypt to dream and blocked him from understanding it. He did all this to set Joseph up for his breakthrough moment. If you take pleasure in interpreting other people's dreams, your life will not remain the same. Palace doors will open unto you because you have pursued wisdom and discernment. The Lord will set you over every kingdom because your time has come.

Pharaoh had to tell Joseph that, "only in the throne will I be greater than you." This was the same Joseph that went through preparation in the pit, in Potiphar's house, in the prison and now in the palace. This is what I call *The Principle of the 9 P's:*

Proper preparation particularly in pits, prisons and Potiphar's house prevents poor performance.

Joseph acquired the experience to rule over Egypt from his past ordeals. You will rule over the kingdom of your enemy! God will bring you out of the prison you are going through today and he will set you over the land of the enemy.

"And Pharaoh said unto Joseph, See I have set thee over all the land of Egypt. And Pharaoh took of his ring from his hand and put it upon Joseph's hand, and arrayed him in vestures of fine linen, and put a gold chain about his neck; And he made him to ride in the second chariot which he had; and they cried before him, Bow the knee: and he made him ruler over all the land of Egypt" (Genesis 41:41-43).

Those who think they have done evil to you by taking your coat of many colours are actually preparing you for your royal apparel. When the enemy takes your coat, the Lord will give you a ring of royalty. The enemy can take your coat but he cannot take your dream. Do not allow anyone to steal your dream or vision. Your vision is your visa to success; your vision is your motivator. You must protect your vision and dream at all times.

It does not take God more than a minute to turn your situation around. He will take the toil away, change your raiment, change the people around you and will dress you in royal apparel.

Pharaohs do not remove their ring to give to ordinary people. However, when your ultimate breakthrough comes, God will alter the order and counter the procedures.

What qualifies you to experience an ultimate breakthrough is your ability to endure hardness without revenge. Do not revenge just because power is in your hands. When you are tempted to fight back at the moment of your ultimate breakthrough, restrain yourself and think of your coming glory.

Joseph refused to revenge his brothers because he knew that vengeance is the Lord's. If the Lord is fighting on your behalf, do not take over the fight from him. Joseph had to deny his flesh to enjoy divine elevation. If you must enjoy divine elevation, die to your past. As you enter your ultimate breakthrough, enter with the fear of the Lord because it takes only one day for everything below you to come over you.

Saviour of the World

"And Pharaoh said unto Joseph, I am Pharaoh, and without thee shalt no man lift up his hand or foot in all the land of Egypt. And Pharaoh called

Joseph's name Zaphnath-paaneah; and he gave him to wife Ase-nath the daughter of Poti-pherah priest of On. And Joseph went out over all the land of Egypt" (Genesis 41:45).

The name Zaphnath-paaneah means Savior of the world. What people call you will dictate who you are and the problem you have come to solve in their lives. The names they call you are just the confirmation of what God has ordained in your life. True success can be seen in your ability to forget the past.

You Are Not An Exception

"And Joseph called the name of the firstborn Manasseh: for God, said he, hath made me forget all my toil, and all my father's house. And the name of the second called he Ephraim: for God hath caused me to be fruitful in the land of my affliction" (Genesis 41:51,52).

At your ultimate breakthrough level, it is important that you get your priorities right. Joseph, at the peak of his victory named his two sons according to his life encounter and eventual breakthrough. He named the first, "Manasseh" which means "God has made me forget all my toil." His second child was named "Ephraim," meaning "God has made me fruitful in the land of my affliction".

However, Jacob, Joseph's father, full of age and wisdom, rearranged the destiny of these children by setting "Ephraim" before "Manasseh". Joseph was not pleased when he saw his father laying his right hand on the younger and the left hand on the older (Genesis 48:13-18). Nonetheless, his great and affectionate mentor displayed much wisdom by this prophetic act.

At the ultimate zone, be careful not to disobey your mentor. He may not always do what pleases you but he will always do the right thing.

"And his father refused, and said, I know it, my son, I know it: he also shall become a people, and he also shall be great: but truly his younger brother shall be greater than he, and his seed shall become a multitude of nations. And he blessed them that day, saying, in thee shall Israel bless, saying, God make thee as Ephraim and as Manasseh: and he set Ephraim before Manasseh". (Genesis 48:19-20).

Good advice will help you to do the right thing at the right time and in the right way. If *Ephraim* means, "God has made me fruitful in the land of my affliction" and *Manasseh* means "God has made me forget my toil", then setting your

Ephraim before Manasseh is absolute, because, *it is when you become fruitful that you can forget your toil*. Once you enter your ultimate breakthrough, you will forget the sorrow of yester years.

Get it right.   You have to experience your "Ephraim" before your "Manasseh;" and this will happen at your Ultimate Breakthrough zone.

Name your trouble; put a tag on it; leave it in the past, and move on.   It is not the end of the world; the Lord is turning your situation around.

"For ye shall go out with joy, and be led forth with peace: the mountains and the hills shall break forth before you into singing, and all the trees of the field shall clap their hands." (Isaiah 55:12).

The mountains in your life will bow and fall down.   They will give way and every problem that seems insurmountable will bow down to you. You will overcome all problems in Jesus name. When you get to the ultimate, problems begin to give way, those who hate you will become the ladder you will climb to your success.

"Sing, O ye heavens; for the Lord had done it: Shout, ye lower parts of the earth: Break forth into singing, ye mountains, O forests, and every

tree therein: for the Lord had redeemed Jacob and glorified himself in Israel." (Isaiah 44:23).

Finally, never give up before your ultimate breakthrough comes. Those who give up are given off as prey to the terrorising lion of their lives called "failure".

I agree with you in prayer right now: *Your moment of ultimate breakthrough has come; you will arise and shine for your light has come and the glory of God is risen upon your life. You will not only be an observer but a preserver because not all observers are preservers but all preservers are observers. Begin to go from victory to victory as you continue to hold the fort. No evil person shall stand before you, and every tongue that rises against you in judgment, you will condemn. No weapon fashioned against you shall prosper. You will discover your wings and soar like eagles. Enjoy every moment of your Ultimate Breakthrough, holding the fort and keeping an intimate relationship with the God of wonders.*

Amen.

WISDOM PRINCIPLES

*God is not a respecter of persons
but a respecter of principles.*

*The condition for reaping the harvest
is to "faint not."*

*Jesus was crowned with the crown of thorns so that
you can be crowned with the crown of life.*

*To get to the height of success is not a problem
but the character to sustain you there.*

*When you struggle in your strength,
you put God to rest but when you enter into His rest,
you put God to work.*

*Arriving at the top of the mountain is not the end of
the world because to descend is much easier.*

*When God is with you,
you will move from grass to grace.*

*Success is not success without accomplishing
God's divine purpose in your life.*

Only the broken become masters at mending.

*Personal testimony is a master key
to releasing faith in others.
Let your lifestyle be a testimony to others.*

*Never lose your guard at the ultimate
breakthrough, always seek divine reinforcement.*

*For you to enjoy your progress to the ultimate,
you need a strong personal relationship with God;
do not wait for corporate anointing.*

*You need to be connected to heaven at all times;
your connection to heaven is the main
determinant of your progression in life.*

*Do not let your title rob you of your entitlement before
the Lord. Your title has no rating before God;
it is only recognized by men.*

Yesterday's strategy is too old for today's battle.

*Proper preparation particularly in pits, prisons and
Potiphar's house prevents poor performance.
The taking of your coat of many colours
prepares you for a royal apparel.*

*Your qualification for an ultimate breakthrough is the
ability to endure hardness without revenge.*

*The names people call you are just the
confirmation of what God has done in your life.*

*True success can be seen
in your ability to forget the past.*

THE FLOODGATES OF BLESSING

(Maximising Your Ultimate Breakthrough)

At last! You are now here—at the point of your ultimate breakthrough! Your life has changed completely and you are enjoying the blessings of the Lord. Your adversaries can clearly see the grace of God upon you and they are all at peace with you. You have ceased from your works and the Lord is causing all things to work for your good. Indeed, your life can never be the same again!

Purpose of Breakthrough

It is important, at this stage of your journey, to understand God's purpose in blessing you. His words to Abraham was, "I will bless thee... and thou shalt be a blessing" (Genesis 12:3). God's purpose for bringing you to your moment of ultimate breakthrough is for you to be a channel of blessing to others. He has not blessed you just for yourself, but also for others around you.

David knew this purpose very well. He was not selfish with God's blessing in his life. He had a giving attitude that blessed the nation. He was even ready to bless his enemies:

"And David said, Is there yet any that is left of the house of Saul, that I may shew him kindness for Jonathan's sake?" (2 Samuel 9:1).

This attitude to bless gave Mephibosheth, Jonathan's son, access to the king's table—even though he was lame in both feet (2 Samuel 9:13).

At your ultimate breakthrough zone, God will expect you to bless your enemies. You may not feel doing it but obey the word of God.

"Bless them which persecute you: bless, and curse not... Recompense to no man evil for evil... Dearly beloved, avenge not yourselves, but rather give place unto wrath for it is written,

Vengeance is mine; I will repay saith the Lord. Therefore if thine enemy hunger, feed him; if he thirst, give him drink: for in so doing thou shalt heap coals of fire on his head. Be not overcome with evil, but overcome evil with good" (Romans 12:14,17,19-21).

God also wants you to be a financier in His kingdom. If you do not acknowledge the Source of your breakthrough, your breakthrough can break apart. David's attitude at his ultimate breakthrough was not to offer God anything that would cost him nothing (2 Samuel 24:24).

In appreciation to the God of his breakthrough, David thought of ways to be a blessing to the house of God. When God saw the attitude of David, He opened the floodgates of heaven's blessing upon David and established his dynasty for a thousand generations.

"And it came to pass, when the king sat in his house, and the Lord had given him rest round about from all his enemies; that the king said unto Nathan the prophet, See now, I dwell in an house of cedar, but the ark of God dwelleth within curtains. And Nathan said to the king, Go, do all that is in thine heart; for the Lord is with thee. And it came to pass that night, that the word of the Lord came unto Nathan saying,

Go and tell my servant David, Thus saith the Lord, Shalt thou build me an house for me to dwell in? Whereas I have not dwelt in any house since the time that I brought up the children of Israel out of Egypt, even to this day, but have walked in a tent and in a tabernacle. In all the places wherein I have walked with all the children of Israel spake I a word with any of the tribes of Israel, whom I commanded to feed my people Israel, saying, Why build ye not me an house of cedar? Now therefore so shalt thou say unto my servant David, Thus saith the Lord of hosts, I took thee from the sheepcote, from following the sheep, to be ruler over my people, over Israel: And I was with thee whithersoever thou wentest, and have cut off all thine enemies out of thy sight, and made thee a great name, like the name of the great men that are in the earth. Moreover I will appoint a place for my people Israel, and will plant them that they may dwell in a place of their own, and move no more; neither shall the children of wickedness afflict them any more as beforetime. And as since the time that I commanded judges to be over my people Israel, and have caused thee to rest from all thine enemies. Also the Lord telleth thee that he will make thee an house. And when thy days be fulfilled and thou shalt sleep with thy fathers, I will set up thy seed after thee, which shall proceed out of

thy bowels, and I will establish his kingdom. He shall build an house for my name, and I will stablish the throne of his kingdom forever." (2 Samuel 7:1-13).

This is nothing less than the floodgates of blessing and it was triggered by David's generosity towards the Lord's house. This overflowing blessing affected not only David but also his son and the whole nation of Israel.

Even though you are experiencing blessing at your ultimate breakthrough zone, there is still more you can unlock by becoming a generous giver. You will discover that you cannot out-give God. When you give Him a bucket of blessing, He will open the floodgates of heaven and pour you out a blessing that you cannot contain by yourself; others will be needed, even future generations, to contain the blessing.

Floodgates

Let us gain some wisdom about how God intends to bless us from the nature of floods.

A flood is an unlimited, unrestrained, unhindered and irresistible force that forces everything on its way to move with it. A flood cannot be contained. When there is a flood in a place, everyone around is affected.

A flood is greater than trickles, gushes or even outpours. Indeed, the floodgate of blessing is the desire of everyone (no one has ever had enough blessing to say he does not want some more).

The floodgate of God's blessing that is available for you is not from man, but from above. It is an open heaven that releases diverse kinds of blessing from the Lord.

When the heavens are open on a man, the promises in Deuteronomy 28:1-14 comes to pass in his life. When the heavens open, the glory of God comes down and no negativity or failure can prevail the life of the person. If you can learn the wisdom of David and do the things that he did, the heavens will open over you.

Open an Account in the Bank of Heaven

If you want the floodgates of heaven to open upon you, lay up your treasure above where there can be no destruction on it (Matthew 6:19-21). The floodgates of blessing cannot open to you unless you are ready to receive of it. To show that you are ready to receive of the floodgates of blessings then you must be ready to totally submit yourself to God and be ready to lay up treasure in heaven. The floodgates of heaven cannot open unto you unless you have laid up treasure above. Therefore God is expecting you to lay up for yourself treasures in heaven so that you can receive an opening of financial doors on earth.

In other words, the floodgates of blessing cannot be opened unto you unless you obey the laws of giving and receiving. For you to receive, you must give.

A release from the floodgates of blessings can only come as a result of your obedience to God when you have to make sacrifices. You must be able to sacrifice to God with everything. You should give God the tithe of your money, time, resources and everything you have. This is because you know that everything you are and desire to be is through Him. All your achievements came by the special grace of God.

The floodgate of God's blessing does not pertain to material things alone. Rather, it is all encompassing. It will affect every area of your life.

Absolute Obedience is Necessary

If the floodgates of heaven will open over you, obedience is necessary. Absolute blessings is a result of absolute obedience. You get absolute blessings by re-investing what God has given you into the kingdom of God. If you are willing and obedient, you shall eat the good of the land.

"Ye are cursed with a curse for ye have robbed me, even this whole nation. Bring ye all the tithes into the storehouse that there may be meat in mine house, and prove me now herewith saith the Lord of hosts, if I will not open the windows of heaven, and pour out a blessing that there will be not enough room to receive it." (Malachi 3:9).

The secret key for entering your breakthrough is when you are in absolute obedience to God's instructions concerning your tithes and offerings.

The Law of Tithing

God does not expect us to negotiate our tithes with Him. He requires us to give Him *all* that belongs to Him. God does not need your money but he wants you to give Him a tenth of everything. If you want heaven's floodgates you must be ready to give all to Him.

"And [Abraham] gave him tithes of all" (Genesis 14:20).

It is clear that God will provide for His work with or without our tithe. However, it is not possible for us to receive His best if we do not obey Him in the tithe.

Listen, the beauty of an environment does not beautify your life. The only thing that beautifies you is your personal obedience to what God says about you. You need to give tithes for everything in your life so that your ultimate breakthrough can outlast you and the coming generations.

You are not a covenant-keeping child of God if you cannot obey Him in the tithe. When you identify your purpose on earth and utilise the gifts of God in your life, be ready also to give out of what you have received. This is the secret of continuous receiving.

You cannot say you love God without giving to Him. There is no loving without giving. When you love God, you would follow Him. Job loved God and vowed to trust God even if God slays him. It was your love for God that helped you through the dark seasons of life. Now that you are at your ultimate breakthrough, do not stop loving God. Give all the tithes to Him.

Tithing Your Money

Your tithe of money is the kind that can give you financial breakthrough. Money is just an errand boy; it is not supposed to have dominion over you. You should possess money without money possessing you. If God gives you a little and you are unfaithful with it, do not expect Him to release you into the realm of abundant breakthrough.

You must be able to invest into the kingdom of God. If God releases you to your preliminary breakthrough and you are unfaithful there, would you expect God to release you into your ultimate breakthrough?

The keys to opening the floodgates of blessing are in your hands. You should pay a gross tithe instead of a net tithe. Your prayers cannot make you rich if you do not pay your tithe.

Listen, God wants you to honor Him with your substance because when you honor Him, He will give you a substantial blessing.

Do not give leftovers to God; always set apart what belongs to God. Do not treat God with levity, neither give to Him what you cannot give to your governors. Amend your ways so that God can open the floodgates of heaven over you.

5 Blessings of the Tithe

The following are five blessings of the tithe that are contained in Malachi 3:9,10.

1. Open Heaven

"I will open the windows of heaven"

This is the time God will lift you into the realm of possibilities and everything begins to prosper without sweat or stress.

This is when blessings come your way and right things come at the right time. Doors of connections are opened to you and great ideas begin to come.

When the floodgate of blessing is open, it sweeps you off your feet and causes you to stagger. This is the blessing that will make people rush to bless you. It is the level where people begin to use your identity for breakthrough. Even doors are opened without your appearance.

2. Showers of Blessing

"And I will pour you out a blessing"

God wants you to experience more than a trickle of His blessings; He wants you to experience the mighty showers that pour without restrain. There are lots of ideas in you that have the potential to yield great returns but there is nothing greater than the outpouring of God's blessings that can make them effective.

Are you fed up of trickles of the rain of blessings? Then begin to expect the showers of God's blessings by giving your all to God.

3. No More Losses

"And I will rebuke the devourer for your sake, and he shall not destroy the fruits of your ground"

When the devourer is in someone's finances, such a person will not be able to account for his spending. But when the Lord rebukes the devourer, decisions will be well calculated and there will be no more losses.

Instead of allowing the devourer to waste your finances, obey God and He will rebuke the devourer for your sake. The devourer comes as a result of decisions that are not well taken or the impromptu expenses that are not budgeted for, such as sudden sickness, death, and swindles. The devourer is all out to eat people's work, peace, finances, livelihood, and blessings. You can reverse this condition by being generous towards God's house.

4. Matured/Well-Built Success

"Neither shall your vine cast her fruit before the time in the field, saith the Lord of hosts".

When the Lord rebukes the devourer for your sake, you will not have insignificant blessings but mature and well-built blessings that will sweep the enemy off his feet. The bible promises that when you pay your tithe, your vine will not be cast before their time. This means that when your vine is cast in time you will have no losses or premature blessings.

This also means that the Lord will exalt you and you will work according to God's divine timing and have his divine favour.

5. A Source of Blessing

"And all nations shall call you blessed; for you shall be a delightsome land".

When God blessed Abraham, he did not only bless Abraham with physical things but also made him a blessing to others. As we noted earlier, it is not enough to be blessed; it is more important to be a blessing. Nations will call you blessed because you have been a blessing to them. People and nations will delight in you because you have given them something to delight in.

At your ultimate breakthrough zone, blessings perpetuate with or without your appearance in a place. Other people get blessed as a result of their association with you. When God makes you a source of blessing, you do not need to fear or fret because you are already approved of God;

your blessing cannot be covered up or hindered; it is a blessing that has been made manifest for all to see — an open breakthrough that nobody can disrupt.

Without any doubt, this is what God intends for your life. Your journey does not end at the moment of ultimate breakthrough. It starts there. May your life become a source of blessing to many. You will lend to nations and not borrow. You will overflow with the floods of God's blessing and generations after you will call you blessed. Amen.

WISDOM PRINCIPLES

Putting new wine in an old bottle will make you lose both the wine and the bottle so why not break the old bottle and save the new wine.

A release from the floodgates of blessings can only come as a result of your obedience to God – the laws of giving and receiving.

Ultimate breakthrough is not only in material things but rather it is all encompassing.

Ultimate breakthrough is absolute blessings, which is a result of absolute obedience.

If you want to enter your ultimate breakthrough then you must be ready to give all to Him.

You cannot out-give God.

The beauty of an environment does not beautify your life; the only thing that beautifies you is your personal obedience to what God says to you.

You cannot say you love God without giving to Him,
there is no loving without giving
(but there is giving without loving).

You should have money
instead of money having you.

Unfaithfulness in your preliminary breakthrough
will disqualify you for an ultimate breakthrough.

When you honor God with your substance,
He will give you a substantial blessing.

STRICTLY FOR
LANDING PASSENGERS!

Without an iota of doubt, I am convinced that this book has been a great blessing to you. A visa to your *Moment of Ultimate Breakthrough* has been issued and you have boarded, through this book, the flight to greatness.

I will love to hear from you and receive you at the height of your breakthrough. It would be deeply appreciated if you communicate with me through the address on the next page. Let me know your testimonies and share in your joy. Be assured that our hands are continually open to offer counseling and to receive your prayer requests.

Hear this in closing, *"And it shall come to pass in the last days, that the mountain of the Lord's house shall be established in the top of the mountains, and shall be exalted above the hills; and all nations shall flow unto it (Isaiah 2:2).* See you at top for that is where you belong.

God bless you.

- Ebenezer Ajitena

Ebenezer Ajitena
CLIWOM Sanctuary of Praise
709 Old Kent Road
London SE15 1JL
Tel/Fax: (+44) 020 7358 9994
Tel: (+44) 020 7358 9992
Email: ajitena@hotmail.com

CLIWOM SANCTUARY OF PRAISE
is a full liberation ministry and a church where
we share the vision of success with the
people of destiny.